Principles of Black Political Economy

External/Internal Labor Process

Pol. Eco. def, p.12

Principles of Black Political Economy

Lloyd Hogan

Routledge & Kegan Paul
Boston, London, Melbourne and Henley

First published in 1984
by Routledge & Kegan Paul plc

9 Park Street, Boston, Mass. 02108, USA

39 Store Street, London WC1E 7DD, England

464 St Kilda Road, Melbourne,
Victoria 3004, Australia and

Broadway House, Newtown Road,
Henley-on-Thames, Oxon RG9 1EN, England

Set in 10/12pt Linotron Sabon
by Input Typesetting Ltd, London
and printed in the United States of America

Copyright © Lloyd Hogan 1984

No part of this book may be reproduced in
any form without permission from the publisher,
except for the quotation of brief passages
in criticism

Library of Congress Cataloging in Publication Data

Hogan, Lloyd L.
Principles of Black political economy.
Bibliography: p.
Includes index.
1. Economics.   2. Afro-Americans—Economic conditions.
3. Blacks—Economic conditions.   I. Title.   II. Title:
Black political economy.
HB171.5.H683   1984   330.973'008996073   83–21240

ISBN 0–7102–0177–X (c)
ISBN 0–7102–0241–5 (p)

AFFECTIONATELY DEDICATED TO

A family that typifies black population continuity

> My mother, Kathleen (1895–1971)
> My father, Leonard (1893–1958)
>   who are no more
>
> My wife, Elsie
>
> Our children
> Indira, Pauli, Bena, Kamala, Vijaya,
> Shiva, Milo, Diallo
>
> the children of our children
> Yusuf, Malaika, Rahsaan, Tahirah, Salim,
> Munera, Nujaima, Hamza, Kamau, Shomari
>   and others to come
>
> and
>
> the children of our children's children
>   who are yet to be born

CONTENTS

	Preface	ix
	Introduction	1
1	The general nature of political economy	9
2	Special types of political economies	36
3	Special cases of black American political economies	70
4	African origins of black Americans, 1450–1865	78
5	The system of black slave labor and the rise of capitalism in Western Europe, 1619–1865	84
6	The black sharecropping system and the development of capitalism in the United States, 1865–1965	102
7	The black wage labor system and the rate of capital accumulation in the United States, 1965–	115
8	The role of black Americans in the social reconstruction of the future	163
	Notes and suggested reading	172
	Bibliography	177
	Index	179

PREFACE

The current state of the discipline of political economy as taught in institutions of higher learning is rather trivial at best and downright dangerous at worst. The burning theoretical issues dealt with and the corresponding methodology provide a series of rationalizations which justify the existing conditions in which wage workers find themselves.

The treatment of blacks is even more deplorable. Blacks were not considered to be a legitimate subject matter for study and were thus completely ignored until the middle 1950s. The publication of Becker's book initiated a floodtide of articles in the leading journals on the "economics of discrimination." During Johnson's so-called "war on poverty" another spate of books, articles, and pamphlets came off the presses in rapid-fire fashion. Financing of these publications generally came out of the very war chest which was to help blacks and other poor people. Many of these productions were either irrelevant to the issues facing black people in the United States, or they developed more efficient methods of suppressing the legitimate aspirations of blacks and the poor.

These publications, however, helped to build a reputation for a number of white scholars and their affiliated institutes. White experts on black economic problems multiplied rapidly. Private and public research grants have since been aggrandized by these experts and their institutes. The irony is that, at one such institute which receives the lion's share of National Science Foundation grants to do research on poor people and blacks, practically no black scholar has been involved in the work. The old and time-worn excuse of former racist employers that it is difficult to attract black scholars is still used.

Preface

There does not now exist a single textbook devoted to a black political economy. Samuelson's elementary text – the dominant standard for more than three decades – deals with blacks as an afterthought of one chapter on women and minorities. There is no alternative written by a black author which can be used as a basis for an elementary or intermediate course. This makes it difficult to develop a good course without one book of "principles" which may serve as a guide to students in this field.

This book is written with the express purpose of filling the void. It has been long in the making, beginning about four decades ago, when as an undergraduate student at a leading university, I found it necessary to pursue a series of independent studies in the economic development of black people in the United States. There was absolutely nothing in the official curriculum that was useful. In the general social science courses blacks were treated in the most trivial, if not racist, ways. The "economics" courses were totally useless as instruments for analyzing the black condition. In graduate school it was academic suicide to even suggest that a scientific treatment of any "black" economic issue could solve some of the methodological flaws in the discipline.

The actual preparation of the book developed from specific attempts during the last thirty years to bring substance and meaning to the teaching of courses in economics. At some of the predominantly black colleges I found students to be totally turned off with the standard fare. At predominantly white colleges, on the other hand, I found an inordinate amount of student anxiety if there were any departures from the standard materials. The solution was to frame the study in such a way that it encompassed the general problems of economic development of the United States, while at the same time treating the problems of black people as an important subset of the larger economy in which they are embedded.

The book is designed for serious black students of political economy. Black high schools and undergraduate students have no single text in this field that treats them as the central core of study. I hasten to admit at once that this first attempt may not be immediately usable by such students. Therefore, I am hoping that my black colleagues – those with graduate degrees in "economics" and in all of the other social sciences – will make use of the book as an important resource in their courses. I also hope that white economists will at least use the book as an alternative mode of thought about the structure and functioning of the political economy.

In the preparation of this book I relied heavily on three of my best teachers, two of whom I never met in person, and one whom I came to know on a personal level only for an extremely short period of time. Adam Smith laid the foundations for my understanding of the general nature of political economy. Karl Marx provided the more rigorous scientific foundations as well as the passionate commitment to the interests of the working classes. Finally, my everlasting gratitude must go out to the great W. E. B. Dubois, whose analyses of the nature of human society and of the people that make it up have been unparalleled in the history of higher learning.

My wife, Elsie, deserves special mention. She has tolerated my persistent recitals of the materials in this volume for decades without complaint. I couldn't have completed the book without her encouragement and sympathetic criticisms.

Some of my colleagues have read the manuscript and have been quite helpful in suggesting important revisions of substance and clarity. Douglas Davidson of the Institute of the Black World in Atlanta, Georgia must be singled out for my special thanks. His detailed critique has been most useful in sharpening my understanding of some of the more controversial aspects of the work.

Michael Whitter of the University of the West Indies in Mona, Jamaica has painstakingly gone through the manuscript in a most critical way, suggesting a number of significant changes that would make the book more scientifically sound. He has my gratitude for his patience and understanding, even when I failed to take his good advice.

Robert Browne has had a greater influence on my thinking than he is probably aware of. The many years of our close personal friendship, our sharing of ideas as fellow students at a midwestern university, and our mutual tenure at the Black Economic Research Center in Harlem, New York have indeed been of inestimable advantage to me in upgrading my knowledge of the black condition in the United States and in Africa.

My students at Hampshire College have been useful as a standing forum for discussion of the materials in the book. Two of these students, however, stand above all others as critics and co-teaching

Preface

colleagues. Jon Diamond and Jae Jin Shim have been consummate undergraduates who are responsible for making many of the difficult parts of the book more communicable to serious students at all levels of training. I owe them my thanks.

A host of other colleagues have been most helpful. Their names would fill a whole volume. Needless to say, I am grateful to all of them for the contributions they have made to improve the presentation of the materials of this book. However, I must take full responsibility for whatever wrong-headed ideas and faulty conclusions are put forth in the work.

Hampshire College
Amherst, Massachusetts

INTRODUCTION

The central theme of the book is that black Americans are fundamentally no different from any other people. Indeed, their history reflects a pattern of economic development which is quite consistent with the changing social-economic fortunes of all peoples throughout human history. Moreover, during the last five and a half centuries those people who are now identified as black Americans have played a most decisive role in the origins of capitalism as well as the rate and geographic extent of its development in the world.

The dominant factor in their history to date has been the exploitation of their labors by an alien people under three distinct historical modes of social-economic organization — slavery, sharecropping, and wage laboring. During the interval of real time during which blacks experienced each of these three historical epochs, members of the general American working class were exploited under a different form of political economy. Thus, it has come to appear that there is some inherent "racial" character which sets black Americans apart from non-black workers in the American social setting.

Implicit throughout the book is the thesis that only an insignificant, but very powerful, number of non-blacks have been responsible for the material poverty of blacks in each of the three epochs. The other non-black members of the population, who constitute the overwhelming majority, have been, to varying degrees, used by the ruling classes as the direct subjective instruments of black exploitation; and this has been made possible as a consequence of the fundamental institutional mechanisms by which these non-blacks were made to survive. As such, these non-black workers

Introduction

have been also the ready victims of labor exploitation, even if under a different type of political economy than their black counterparts.

A crucial element of the overall theme is that black people have played the most decisive role in liberating themselves in the past from slavery and from sharecropping modes of exploitation and that they will liberate themselves again in the future from the present-day wage laboring exploitative system. Liberation from any existing mode of labor exploitation is a function of that very mode of exploitation itself. Indeed, we shall argue that the intensity and extent of exploitation of the labor of black people in the production of the material means of their survival necessarily calls into play a corresponding intensity and extent of labor of black people to maintain their living status and to survive as a population. Progressive expansion in these two phases of black human effort over time ultimately generates a sufficiently explosive social force which blasts asunder the shackles of the distributive mechanisms that legitimately enforce the existing mode of black human labor exploitation. When this event occurs, the system of political economy is transformed into a new system.

The organizing principle of the book, therefore, is the analysis of the alternating phases of black human labor – the one external to the black population, resulting in the creation of the material means of survival; the other internal to the black population, resulting in the creation of the black population itself. To complete the analysis we shall have to specify the nature of the distributive mechanisms which legitimately set the preconditions under which these two phases of black human labor may take place. But the completion of each cycle of black human labor requires the existence of a social switching mechanism to restart the cycle under exactly the same social arrangements as before. We shall locate this mechanism in the process of accumulation of wealth in a form characteristic of the historical epoch in which black human labor is being generated.

These themes and organizing principles suggest that we are essentially dealing with issues in social reproduction. Black human labor is the crucial activity; the simultaneous but sequential destruction and creation of black people and the means of black human survival are the intermediary outcomes; net reproduction of the black population is the final material outcome.

Existing studies in black political economy have generally been

Introduction

compendiums of factual information on employment, income differentials, poverty, educational attainment, rampant racism within the general white population, government social programs, national political participation, and a host of otherwise unrelated phenomena. Our basic theme of black population reproduction should enable us to better organize the data in a more consistent manner than heretofore.

The major objective of the book is the construction of a theoretical framework for explaining the mechanisms by which the black population of the United States reproduces itself as a black population. Who they are today and what survival strategies keep breath in their bodies are consequences of a set of historical forces which generated them out of some primordial earth matter about three million years ago, propelled them through many and varied social-economic formations, and finally solidified their present defining characteristics as well as their physical location within the bowels of the most powerful capitalist nation that the world has ever known.

The methodology of political economy is quite appropriate to the task at hand. On our view, the central focus of political economy is the social reproduction of a human population. This contrasts with individual reproduction in the sense that it is the maintenance of the population as a population (and not as a mere collection of individuals) with all its important characteristics remaining intact.

The act of individual reproduction – the birthing of babies out of the sexual synthesis of adult male and female people – is a necessary condition for social reproduction to occur; but it is not a sufficient condition. Social reproduction encompasses much more. It entails the complex set of interrelations that link the individual members of the human population, one to another, in stable and regularly recurring bonds of co-operative existence.

At the very instant of birth, the social dimensions of the new baby's existence become evident. It is at once the offspring of two adult members of the population; thus it forms a link in the past history of its progenitors. It is also at once an integral member of a family; as such, it partakes immediately in all those activities which make for the reproduction of that family as an integral member of its population group. Finally, it plays a fundamental role as replacement for some member of the population outside of its own family structure who succumbed to death, or it serves as

Introduction

raw material fodder out of which the physical substrata of the population are formed, or it constitutes a net addition to the surviving population as a whole. One live birth therefore gets intertwined in the creation of the fundamental elements of the population, in the decay or death of those same elements of the population, and in the future survival and growth of that population.

In the ensuing years after birth this newborn baby must be reared to full adulthood; it must be "socialized"; it must be wrought and forged into a form that is peculiar to the population as a whole. It must have impressed into its subconscious mind a common language, religion, art, literature, music, mythology. Recreational events, religious rites, formal schooling, informal instruction, political activity, theatrical performances, etc. are some of the instrumentalities used in this regard. Needless to say, the production and consumption of its food supply and other material means of its survival are important aspects of the socialization process. A baby does not live by bread alone; but neither can it survive without it.

The standard academic fare in political economy tends to concentrate on the distribution of the material means of the people's survival. Usually, some lip-service is given over to discussions of the production of the material means of survival. In any case, other aspects of social reproduction are usually ignored, under the pitiful excuse that "they will be held constant for purposes of the analysis." In our study of black people, however, we cannot afford to hold anything constant. The influences which have operated on them have been total. If, in this work, we merely skim the surface of some of the important aspects of black people's social reproduction it will not be because we have deliberately ignored them; responsibility for such omission will be due to our own lack of competence to deal scientifically with the detailed workings of certain reproductive activities traditionally dealt with by social scientists outside the realm of political economy.

Throughout their history, the lot of black Americans has been dictated by the interests of an alien marauder. Their will has been bludgeoned and coerced under some of the most vicious forms of human exploitation ever inflicted upon one people by another. The consequent expenditure of their labor and their bodies and their souls, in desperate attempts to be liberated from the shackles of

Introduction

oppression and to survive as a distinctive black population, is without parallel in world history. Their material poverty has been a vivid memorial of its opposite – the extraordinary quantity of material wealth which their labors have produced and which has been stolen from them throughout the ages. This poverty has also been a visible manifestation of the intensity and agony of their labors in the production and rearing of their children to full adulthood. The relatively large number of black babies necessarily given birth by them, the correspondingly large number of dead black bodies that are necessary to serve as raw material fodder out of which the physical substrata of the black population are created, and the relatively small number of black survivors which results from these two preceding events are dramatic testimonials to the extent and agony of black social reproduction.

The underlying theme of the book is that the black experience has been an essential link in the events which have dominated the world from the middle of the fifteenth century to the present. It has been a most important factor in the origins and development of capitalism in Western Europe and its offshoots in North America. As such, the appropriate framework for explaining the otherwise complex aspects of black social reproduction is the same framework which explains the origin and development of capitalism in the world. The book is structured in such a way as to illuminate the main theme.

The main contribution of this work to an understanding of political economy is the conception of human labor as two continuous, synchronized, and complementary alternating phases of the most fundamental activity that drives the political economy. The literature acknowledges the role of only one phase of human labor – that which we shall refer to throughout this work as External Labor. This is the phase of human labor which uses up (consumes) human energy (and consequently, human beings themselves) in the process of creation of non-human material products. In this work we shall include in the analysis the other, complementary, phase of human labor – that which we shall refer to as Internal Labor. This phase of human labor uses up (consumes) food and other material products in the process of creation of human energy (and consequently, the human carriers of that energy).

On our formulation, the social reproduction of the population

Introduction

involves the unified and continuous performance of both phases of labor. The preconditions for their operation are to be found in the simultaneous and continuing operation of two distributive processes. These latter provide the conduits through which people are distributed from the Internal Labor Process where they are created to the External Labor Process where they are used; and through which material goods are distributed from the External Labor Process where they are created to the Internal Labor Process where they are used. Finally, we bring our analysis to bear on the characteristic process of wealth accumulation which functions as the natural terminus to the complete cycle of labor; but it also functions as the social switching process which restarts the new cycle of labor under the very same conditions as the previous cycle of labor. This process thus insures the continuation of the political economy as the same genre of its origins.

Chapter 1 develops a general model of political economy. It describes the major components and activities which typify any political economy which now exists or has existed in the world. This chapter is quite fundamental to the whole work; it sets the organizational structure of each of the subsequent chapters of the book.

Chapter 2 derives a set of criteria from the general model of Chapter 1 that enables us to describe all the special types of political economies which now exist in the real world or which have existed in the past. This chapter is still of a general mold. It does not discuss any specific people. Nevertheless, it is the essential link with the empirical data. Indeed, it enables us to classify all the peoples of the world into a relatively small subset of types of political economies. Thus, a basis is established for the analysis of any one of these people, including black American people.

Chapter 3 makes use of the models of Chapter 2 by concentrating on a specific people – black Americans – from their origins on earth. It establishes that from such beginnings to the present day they have undergone at least four historical eras in their development; that is to say, four of the special types of political economies identified in Chapter 2 will systematically organize the essential facts of their historical development. Communal beginnings on the continent of Africa up through the middle of the fifteenth century; slave existence from the middle of the fifteenth century to the middle of the nineteenth century; feudal sharecropping existence

Introduction

from the middle of the nineteenth to the middle of the seventh decade of the twentieth century; wage laboring existence from the middle of the seventh decade of the twentieth century to the present – these exhaust their history. The chapter therefore formulates the proper study of black Americans in terms of these four special types of political economies and the nature of the special conditions peculiar to each. A very important aspect of this formulation concerns the persistence of black people throughout all four eras as a people distinguishable from other peoples.

Black people in the United States today come in all the colors of peoples in all the lands of the earth. In order to identify them one has to invoke the facts of their origin on the African continent, their being hunted and conquered and shipped involuntarily across the Atlantic in the holds of the slavers' ships, their being impressed against their natural will into the generation of slave labor in the Americas, their liberation from slavery and their simultaneous impoundment into a class of sharecropping labor, and finally their freedom from the sharecropping system and their simultaneous capture to perform wage labor.

An important consideration in the special cases of black social reproduction is that they have simulated, in a sequential fashion, all but one of the special cases of political economy which have been empirically observed in world history. Thus, it is our hope that the study of black social reproduction will enhance our understanding of the basic principles of political economies in general.

Chapters 4 to 7 develop detailed analyses of each of the four historical eras in black social reproduction. Chapter 4 describes their origins in Africa. It attempts to isolate the reasons why the European marauders were able to destroy the African communal and other pre-capitalist societies and enslave the victims.

Chapter 5 considers the black slaving operations in Africa and across the Atlantic, as well as the black slave labor system in North America, as major factors in the rise and development of Western European and United States capitalism.

Chapter 6 analyzes the black sharecropping system in the southern United States as an important factor in the accumulation of capital wealth, primarily in the northern United States.

Chapter 7 develops a detailed analysis of the black wage labor system throughout the United States and its essential role in providing massive doses of unpaid labor which are materialized as

Introduction

capital wealth in the hands of non-black captains of industry. At the same time, blacks continue to subsist in abject material poverty.

Finally, Chapter 8 attempts to bring together some lessons from the rest of the book to project the future dimensions of black social reproduction.

The book combines a series of methodological tools. It makes use of existence postulates about people, material things, and operational processes which bind the people and the material in ways peculiar to the framework of a particular set of the social reproductive relationships. Certainly, these postulates are quite amenable to empirical refutation. Existing statistical and other observational tools can be invoked in this regard.

We also make use of analytic models explicitly or implicitly stated in Chapter 1. Naturally, some of the more interesting empirical implications of these models are assumed to be true whenever the data to document them are not in hand. The conclusions arrived at on this basis are also subject to empirical refutation.

Finally, we make "novel" interpretations of otherwise widely accepted data. Such interpretations flow naturally from our own analytic models. Much controversy and criticism may be generated by this methodological tactic. Yet, it is precisely such a response that may lead to a revival of interest and study of areas of understanding that heretofore have been closed to further scientific scrutiny by the capitalist academic community.

For those who have an abiding interest in the significance of the black American condition, it is hoped that the work will be found to be of more than passing usefulness.

1 The general nature of political economy

The modern literature produced in mainstream academic institutions has banished the concept of "political economy" into oblivion. Only the so-called radical economists use the concept; but even these rebels exhibit no fundamental differences from their more traditional colleagues.

The concept of "political economy" was used in the pioneering and synthesizing work of the "founding father." Adam Smith's *Wealth of Nations* is the first comprehensive treatise which laid the basis for the discipline. Most of the so-called British classical economists from the middle of the eighteenth century to the end of the nineteenth century continued to make use of the concept in the Smithian sense to guide their studies.

The publication of Alfred Marshall's *Principles* in the last decade of the nineteenth century marked the degeneration of the concept of political economy into the notion of "economics." This new version of the discipline removed itself from the larger dynamics of fundamental social processes and became a study of "the allocation of scarce resources among alternative uses." In capitalist society allocation is accomplished through the instrumentality of market institutions. Thus, the central focus of economics shifted to detailed studies of market forces.

Now, it is obvious that one cannot allocate what does not already exist. It therefore follows that the new formulation ignored the problems of creation of the material means of the people's survival; the creation of the people themselves who are simultaneously subjects, objects, and result of economic activity; the formation and accumulation of material wealth; the transformation of the economy from one form into another; the special roles of

The general nature of political economy

different classes; the role of the political state in maintaining the existing system of political economy; and the nature of impacts of foreign contacts on the domestic economic outcomes.

To be sure, some modicum of effort is given to these topics. However, the human drama is utterly missing. The beginning student becomes overwhelmed with a very sophisticated mathematical and logical apparatus, involving a highly specialized vocabulary, with conclusions stated as precise theorems and laws and principles which must be the envy of the physical scientists.

From the middle of the fourth decade of the twentieth century John Maynard Keynes's *General Theory* shifted emphasis from the role of individuals in market transactions to the strategic function of the political state in driving the economy. The new emphasis was now placed on private capital accumulation, stimulated by public expenditures, taxation, and debt-making in a suitably managed monetary environment.

The class basis of capitalist society was ignored in this new paradigm. Each individual was conceived to be part of a group of savers, or investors, or money speculators. Roles overlap, so that an individual could be a member of two groups or of all three groups at any given moment in time. Similarly, the individual could conceivably move in and out of the various groups over time.

Each group, as a whole, was subject to certain mystical psychological tendencies – propensity to save, propensity to invest, propensity to convert assets into money. Operating in conjunction with these restraints, the political state then pursued fiscal and monetary actions designed to bring about certain predetermined economic results. Expanding national production of material goods under conditions of full employment of human and other resources in a regimen of stable prices could now be guaranteed by the deliberate actions of the political state. The "New Deal" was a monument to this type of economic reasoning.

In recent years the spectacle of rapidly rising prices, rising unemployment of human and other resources, and stagnating national output of material goods occurring simultaneously has called the Keynesian paradigm into question. But Marshall and Keynes have merged in recent years. The modern academic courses and textbooks now divide up the discipline into "micro" and "macro" analysis. The former is Marshall; the latter is Keynes. And the peculiar merger has come about through a branch of the discipline which calls itself "monetary theory."

We cannot generate a programme of study of political economy from the current academic tradition of "economics." We shall try to revert to the classics in order to outline what we believe to be a more fruitful approach toward an understanding of social reality. Our major concern in this work is with black Americans. The traditional view is quite sterile in illuminating the problems of these people. In a more insidious way, the current doctrines have played a not insignificant part in suppressing the aspirations of blacks. Indeed, these doctrines have provided a systematic body of rationalizations which absolve the main enemies of black people of any responsibility for their overt and covert sins. On the other hand, these same rationalizations have placed the onus for the sorry conditions which black people suffer on black people themselves. Explicitly or implicitly, racist doctrines are the results of this body of distortions which pervade the thinking of most Americans and which are skillfully articulated by the educated elite in the land.

In opposition to these views, we proceed to the task of defining what we mean by political economy, so that the remainder of our work will have some measure of systematic guidance. Our formulation will rely heavily on the work of Adam Smith.

> The annual labour of every nation is the fund which originally supplies it with all the necessaries and conveniences of life which it annually consumes....
>
> According therefore, as this produce ... bears a greater or smaller proportion to the number of those who are to consume it, the nation will be better or worse supplied with all the necessaries and conveniences for which it has occasion.

These two short paragraphs contain the basic outline of Smith's conception of political economy. Three fundamental sets of activities by the people are implied. The annual labor of the people creates the material means of their survival. The annual consumption of the material means of survival creates (keeps alive) the people. Finally, the maintenance of a stable relationship between the number of people and the quantity of the material means of survival made available to them for their personal consumption creates wealth.

The general nature of political economy

Smith was also concerned with the origins and development of the capitalist economic system. The historical material of Book III, as well as his comparisons of mercantile capitalism with the so-called agricultural systems in Book IV, gives an indication of his concern with the dynamics of change from one type of system to another.

The role of the political state was crucial in Smith's formulation. In Book V he postulated the fundamental role of the state as the preservation of private property.

> But avarice and ambition in the rich, in the poor the hatred of labour and the love of present ease and enjoyment, are the passions which prompt to invade property, passions much more steady in their operation, and much more universal in their influence. Wherever there is great property, there is great inequality. . . . The affluence of the rich excites the indignation of the poor, who are often both driven by want, and prompted by envy, to invade his possessions. It is only under the shelter of the civil magistrate that the owner of that valuable property . . . can sleep a single night in security.

We shall make use of Smith's conception. However, we shall reinterpret his material in the light of what we have come to know in the more than two centuries which have elapsed since the publication of his book. We shall include in the definition what we believe to be a minimum number of elements, so that we retain some flexibility in its application to the real world. We define the science of political economy as the study of "a human population undergoing the act of social reproduction, over a protracted period of time, under a set of rules promulgated and enforced by a political state, within a bounded geographical domain."

This definition suggests that there are at least six parameters, taken together as a unity, which form the basis for a complete description of a political economy in the real world. These parameters are (a) the geographical space within which the political economy functions, (b) the human population whose social reproduction is the underlying motive force of the political economy, (c) the institutional mechanisms which are the instrumentalities of social reproduction, (d) the historical period during which the people are being reproduced, (e) the political state which oversees the political economy, and (f) the geographical domains outside of the political economy in question.

The geographical domain

The bounded region on the face of the earth within which the people are reproduced is the material site, the base of operations, of the political economy. The region also sets a physical limit to the potential number of economies which may be functioning at any given time. If, for example, we assume that there is a quantum area of earth space necessary for the existence of a political economy, then the potential number of political economies is the physical dimensions of the earth, divided by such a quantum area. This is a crucial observation. The larger the area encompassed by one or more political economies, the smaller is the actual number of political economies throughout the world relative to the potential number capable of existence.

The pristine earth – land, ocean, atmosphere, rivers, lakes, etc. – is the primordial matter out of which both human people and their material means of survival are created. At a more fundamental level, it is the continuously recurring acts of creation, out of earth matter, of human babies and their food supply that form the necessary activities of every conceivable political economy. As such, the geographical domain sets the physical possibilities for the political economy. The climate, weather patterns, physical topography, ocean access, rivers, minerals, soil chemistry, forests, mountains, animals, plants, etc. – all of these things provide the basis for both quantity and form of human and material resources which can be created within the political economy.

We have witnessed throughout history the activities of some people embarking on missions of conquest, slavery, colonization, economic imperialism in order to appropriate for themselves the geographical domains of others. The Western European countries provide a good case in point. For centuries they plundered the earth and its people for their own benefit. Today they do it in more subtle ways through capitalist economic machinations; so that a good part of the earth's population remains in material poverty while a relatively small segment of the people of the northern hemisphere subsists in relative material ease.

In any case, the geographical factor is quite important. It is not only the physical space in which people must operate; it is indeed more significantly the material substratum of the people as well as of their means of survival.

The people

The people constitute the key factor in all political economies. They are the major actors, the subjective elements in the social drama. It is their conscious will that enables them to carry out the essential activities of the system.

The predicate of every political economy is labor. The people drive the system by consciously generating labor, by expending their bodies and souls and energies upon the materials – both human and non-human – of the earth. Thus human labor is the critical activity within the political economy.

The people are also, partly, the objective elements of the political economy. One form of their laboring activity operates upon themselves. The act of consuming the material means of their survival is a necessary part of the mechanisms which ensure their continuity as a people over time.

Finally, the people are, partly, the resulting elements of the system of political economy. It is their reproduction which is the ultimate end of the process.

In summary, the people are subjects, objects and results within the political economy. They are the *dramatis personae* in the social dynamic. They consciously perform the essential acts of laboring upon non-human materials as well as upon themselves. The end result is the reproduction of both the material means of their survival and of themselves.

We shall hereafter refer to the people as the human population. As such, the existence of the people is manifested as an organic whole, as a social entity. While the population is made up of individual human beings, nevertheless it is the existence and interconnections of the individual persons as a cohesive group that are of moment. The population must have a long history of social intercourse in the given geographical domain. Each individual member of the group will expire and vanish from the face of the earth anywhere from zero to one hundred years from birth. On

The general nature of political economy

the other hand, the human population transcends individual lives and continues to survive for hundreds or even thousands of years. It is this protracted existence as a distinctive population, independent of the individual members who make it up, that defines the people.

An important consideration is that the people must have a common history as a people apart from all other people. They must have reproduced themselves as themselves throughout their common historical existence. This implies a continuous process of yielding up their individual existences to the primacy of family relationships. At this level of their being they merge in sexual union and other interpersonal bondings to generate offspring of their own physical human genre and to maintain their lives and social characteristics from birth to full adulthood.

But in the continuing historical drama, under the imperatives of certain social formations, they may even have to yield up the family mode of existence to the primacy of the clan, or the tribe, or the class, or the nation, or the international community. This, of course, will depend upon the rules under which they nurture and grow and socialize their young into the mysteries of their population group.

Commonly accepted modes of communication, education, religion, literature, art, music, politics, recreation, and all other necessary techniques of transforming new babies into members of a distinctive population are the forces at work here. The history of the people *qua* distinctive people is the study which informs this aspect of the political economy. The unique origin, current status, development, transformation, and final outcome are the essential parameters which provide us with a basis for identifying the people within a political economy.

The existence of a political economy presupposes some quantum of people. Precisely what this number is cannot be determined apart from empirical observations of the real world. Fictional accounts tell us of a "Robinson" political economy. But even this individual-based situation didn't last very long. Man Friday soon appeared on the scene. In any case, short of migration into the Robinsonian world from the outside his economy has no future.

Robinson, Adam-Eve, family, clan, tribe, nation, groups of nations in some sort of federation, international community have all been actually observed or have been created in the imagination.

The general nature of political economy

In any case, some set of stable interrelations which join the people in a reproductive mode must persist and must actively function from day to day. Moreover, reproduction entails creating the people anew with all of their physical and social characteristics remaining intact. Reproduction also means that the people persist as a living entity beyond the ravages of time. Once we admit of a limit to the life-span of individuals, we must readily postulate a process of procreation, of birthing of new members to replace those who attain the limiting years of life or those who expire from other causes.

A set of institutions that provide for the reproduction of the people, subject to the constraints of the geographical domain in which they operate, must therefore exist.

Institutional mechanisms of social reproduction

Empirical observations over a wide range of political economies throughout the ages suggest emphatically that certain institutional relationships among the members of the population are absolutely necessary. Indeed, each individual member of the population must be created, must be brought into existence for the first time, by already existing members of that same population. Simultaneously, every already existing member – those who directly participate in creating new members as well as all the others – of that population must be maintained in an active, living status.

In order that these events may take place, every last individual member of the population must daily consume, ingest into herself/himself, a set of non-human earth materials called food. This implies that the food must exist in hand prior to its consumption. Once consumed, the food disappears; but each person's living status is maintained.

The process of consuming the food supply will surely come to an end so soon as that food supply is exhausted. Hence, it follows that there must be a process in daily operation which creates a new stock of food. This is accomplished by the exertion of human effort – the using up of the people's bodies and souls and energies – upon non-human earth matter. This implies that the people must exist prior to their being used up. Once used up, the people expire; but a new supply of food is created.

The general nature of political economy

Now, neither of these two activities can take place over a long period of time unless they are joined together as a unity. The one uses up the food supply, but does not create food. Food must be produced, therefore, from the other process. Similarly, the latter process uses up the people, but does not create people. The people must be produced, therefore, from the former process. Two unifying activities are implied. One supplies food, from the process which produces food, to the process that uses up food; the other supplies people, from the process which creates people, to the process that uses up people.

Finally, there must be a set of activities which operates periodically to accumulate the "excess" people, or the "excess" food, or both. "Excess" refers to the difference between the quantity produced and the quantity consumed within a relevant time period. This set of activities determines the path of development of the political economy, and therefore links its past to its present and to its future.

These considerations give us a fairly precise way of describing in more detail the fundamental nature of the essential institutional mechanisms which determine the process of social reproduction of the population. We shall refer to these as (a) Internal Labor Process, (b) External Labor Process, (c) Process of Distribution of the human population from the Internal Labor Process to the External Labor Process, (d) Process of Distribution of food from the External Labor Process to the Internal Labor Process, (e) Process of Accumulation of Wealth.

The Internal Labor Process

In every conceivable type of human society the survival and growth of the population depend upon the consumption by the people of a food supply. Day in and day out, with relentless regularity, they must ingest into their bodies a certain quantity of food, without which they would soon succumb. Food is the elixir of life, a special subset of the material means of the people's survival. It is capable of being transformed by people into human energy. It is indeed the activity of synthesizing the food with their bodily structures – bones, muscles, skin, nerves, glands, blood, flesh – that fuels the

The general nature of political economy

people with the latent fires that convert them into living agents of labor.

The act of food consumption is the using up, the destruction, of that food supply. Simultaneously, however, this act is also the creation of human energy in the selfsame people who consumed the food. Creative destruction is at play here. Food is destroyed; in a simultaneous sequence, human energy is created. "Transformation" is the key concept. Part of the food which is transformed into human energy may potentially solidify into the bodily structures of the existing members of the population, or into the bodily structures of new additions to the human population. The remaining "free" human energy may be lost to inertia.

We shall hereafter refer to this activity as the Internal Labor Process. It is a labor process inasmuch as it is carried out by human agents. It requires the expenditure of human effort, consciously directed by human beings themselves. It is Internal Labor inasmuch as it is performed on the people themselves. The results of that labor therefore inhere in the people, become an essential characteristic of their very being.

That this process is capable of creating new people should be no mystery. Human energy cannot be created independently of the carriers of that energy. Production of human energy in the existing members of the population maintains them in a living status; production of human energies in the form of a baby crop is an essential condition for the continuity of the population beyond the lifetimes of its individual members.

The family is the fundamental unit of activity within the Internal Labor Process. Such a family is conceived to be a social unit, consisting of at least two adult people, of opposite gender, occupying a common household, co-operatively engaged in the daily consumption of a common food supply, and otherwise co-operatively pursuing the maintenance of their lives. Others may be a part of the family structure. Children who issue from the sexual union between the two original adults, other adults, and other children by "adoption" may enter into the family fold in varying numbers. The key condition is that they all share the common household and the common food supply.

In the language of the mathematician the independent variable in the Internal Labor Process is the family's food supply. Food must be available in the family's household prior to its consumption. But

The general nature of political economy

since food is not produced within the Internal Labor Process, the family's food supply is determined by conditions outside the Internal Labor Process itself. We must emphasize that these conditions may or may not be determined outside the family. We must keep a distinction here between the family as social organization, as potential agent of Internal Labor, on the one hand; and Internal Labor Process as a set of institutional activities carried out by the family. It is a distinction between subject and predicate, between the agency carrying out the activity and the activity itself.

There is a very important subjective element of the Internal Labor Process. This process cannot function unless the people marshall their will consciously to carry out the act of Internal Labor. This conscious will manifests itself in the "intensity" with which that labor is carried out. The "intensity" factor thus becomes another important independent variable. However, it differs from the food variable in that it is determined inside the Internal Labor Process itself. It is the conscious exercise of the people's will that is at issue here. It should be noted that in some societies that will may be the free expression of the people. Still, in other societies that will may be bent and coerced and otherwise controlled by outside forces or outside people. Yet, in all cases it is still the conscious acquiescence of the people which establishes the degree of intensity of Internal Labor.

The result to be achieved is the production of a certain quantity of human energy. Human energy produced is therefore the dependent variable. Since human energy is carried by people, we shall assume that the quantity of human energy produced by a family is directly proportional to the number of family members, including currently born babies.

Let us define the intensity of Internal Labor as the ratio of the number of family members to the quantity of food available to them for consumption. Stated another way, the definition of intensity of Internal Labor is the multiplicative inverse of the food consumption *per capita*. It therefore follows that for any two families with the same quantity of food available, the larger family exerts a greater degree of intensity of Internal Labor. Similarly, for two families with equal number of members, the family with the lesser quantity of food available for consumption exerts a greater degree of intensity of Internal Labor. The upshot of all this is that those families who are blessed with substantial amounts of food

The general nature of political economy

on a *per capita* basis need not exert nearly as much intensity of Internal Labor as those unfortunate families with a pittance of food available to each member.

In summary, it is in the Internal Labor Process that the human population creates itself anew each year. By consuming its food supply it is enabled to maintain the living status of its existing members. But in doing so, it must inevitably create a new baby crop each year. The new babies serve as replacements for those existing members of the population who succumb to death; thus the size of the human population is maintained. In addition, the new babies may also be the basis for growth of the population. Finally, some of these babies may never form a part of the surviving population; they may indeed succumb to forces outside of the Internal Labor Process itself.

(Birthing of babies, nurturing them, amusing them, educating them, politicizing them, mystifying them, moralizing them, socializing them, inculcating into them the mysteries of their peoplehood, rearing them to adulthood – all of these activities are integral parts of the Internal Labor Process.)

Internal Labor Process is the borning ground of the human population. It generates the basis for the surviving population at any given moment in time. It collapses the events of a whole century of population formation into conditions which define the population of the current year. Indeed, the sum total of babies born over the previous one hundred years is the potential population of the current year. Thus, the number of live births during the current year represents the addition to the potential population during the current year. A "law of population production" is therefore embedded in the temporal pattern of annual live births among the various families which make up the human population.

Such a pattern of births can only be known from empirical observations. However, we may still postulate that it can be approximated by two components – a cycle and a time trend. The cycle accounts for the simple replacement of some underlying base year population; the trend accounts for possible annual growth in the potential population.

Babies are born directly into families. The annual total of live births within the Internal Labor Process is therefore the sum total of births within all families. The current distribution of the surviving population among families (denoted by number of members) reflects the surviving residue of the distribution of births. It also reflects the surviving residue of the distribution of human energy produced. Finally, it also reflects the distribution of the quantity of food made available to the various families for their personal consumption. But the surviving population is only a subset of the potential population. The missing component is the number of people who succumb to the ravages of death outside of the Internal Labor Process.

As we have seen, one of the preconditions for the operation of the Internal Labor Process is the existence in the hands of each family of a stock of food. The potential quantity of food in existence within the political economy is the total quantity produced in the current year. The production of the food supply therefore constitutes an important institutional mechanism for social reproduction. We now turn to an examination of the way in which food is produced within the political economy.

The External Labor Process

In all societies throughout the ages the human population must devote some of its time to the production of food. Even in the Garden of Eden, which abounds in the largesse of the deity, poor Adam must spend some time gathering up the fruit. Tilling the soil, fishing the rivers, hunting wild animals, gathering up the fruits of the forests, raising domesticated animals – all of these activities constitute some of the more elementary ways in which humans procure their food supply. Other more elaborate and sophisticated food production activities are possible. Nevertheless, the production of food can be described in a quite general way that applies to all social organizations.

In a fundamental sense the production of food is accomplished by the exertion of human effort against non-human earth matter. The end result is the creation of food, itself a special form of non-human earth matter. What we have here is the using up of human energy, external to the humans themselves, and the simultaneous creation of a food supply. Creative destruction is in operation. Human energies and, consequently, the human carriers of those energies, are destroyed. At the same time, however, a new stock of food is created. In sum, the process is one in which the human

The general nature of political economy

population is transformed into food. This simple activity stands as one of the critical mechanisms for social reproduction.

We shall hereafter refer to this process as the External Labor Process. It is a labor process inasmuch as it is an activity carried out by human people. It is external inasmuch as the people perform the labor activity upon earth matter external to humans. The resulting food produced is thus congealed human External Labor, or what amounts to the same thing, human beings materialized in a special non-human form.

The unit of activity within the External Labor Process differs in different types of social order. In some cases it may involve the entire population upon the virgin land. At the other extreme it may involve one or a few individuals in a business firm. In general, however, the unit of activity is a group, consisting of individuals, working upon the land or upon non-human products of the land, with the conscious aim of creating a food supply.

The process obviously cannot take place without the prior existence of the people, flushed with living energies. But External Labor uses people; it does not create them. Hence, the number of people engaged in External Labor must come from outside the External Labor Process.

The number engaged is the independent variable. However, once involved in the process, nothing can happen unless and until each individual consciously exercises her/his will to produce the food. It is true that the people may be subject to varying degrees of duress; nevertheless, it is still the conscious acquiescence of their will to the tasks at hand that makes External Labor possible.

The conscious exercise of will manifests itself in the "intensity" of External Labor. The "intensity" factor thus becomes a second independent variable in the External Labor Process.

It is obvious that the two independent variables are not independent of each other. Indeed, one is the "number" of people; the other is the conscious will of those same people.

The dependent variable is the quantity of food to be produced. Let us define the intensity of External Labor as the ratio of the quantity of food produced to the number of people directly engaged in producing it. That is to say, intensity of External Labor is food production *per capita*. It then follows that if the same quantity of food is produced by two different units of External Labor, then the unit with the lesser number of people is subject to a greater degree of intensity of External Labor than the unit with the larger number of people. Similarly, if two different units of External Labor engage the same number of people, then the one which produces the larger quantity of food is subject to a greater degree of intensity of External Labor than the one which produces the smaller quantity of food.

We cannot know what quantity of food will be produced in each unit of External Labor without specific empirical observations. Nevertheless, we can postulate that on the level of the entire political economy, the total quantity of food produced must supply the requirements of the Internal Labor Process. This means that it must be directly proportional to the number of people in the surviving human population. But some of the food must also replace the quantity of the existing stocks used up directly in the production of the current food supply. Finally, some may provide for growth in the existing stocks.

At the level of the unit of External Labor we shall assume that similar circumstances prevail. The distribution of food production among these units closely mirrors the distribution of people engaged in its production. Departures from the mirror image are brought about by the effects of the distribution of intensity of External Labor, as well as the distribution of the rate of growth in food production.

The general law of production of the potential food supply may be conceived to consist of two components – a cycle and a time trend. The cycle will account for the continued annual replacement of some base year stock of food; the trend will account for possible growth over time.

We must emphasize the fact that the External Labor Process not only produces the food supply but it does this by using up human energy. As such, it consumes the human population. External Labor Process is therefore the "killing ground" of the human population. The social reproduction of the human population therefore also depends upon the quantity and intensity of External Labor. The specific toll in human lives exacted by the ravages of External Labor is thus one of the more critical factors which must be derived from our empirical studies.

Internal Labor is the borning ground of the human population. It creates the human baby crops. Over the course of a century, these babies form the age distribution structure of the potential

The general nature of political economy

human population during the last year of that century. External Labor, on the other hand, is the killing ground of the human population. Over the course of a century, the dead victims form the temporal distribution of the decayed elements of the potential human population. Finally, the combined effect of the two phases of human labor, enshrined in the distributions of the potential population and the decayed population, is the current age distribution of the surviving human population.

The classical literature in political economy concentrated most of its attention on the External Labor Process. It is obviously quite important, but it certainly cannot function for very long unless it is continuously furnished with fresh supplies of laborers, sated with vital human energies. We must therefore proceed to the task of describing the social mechanism which supplies the human agents of External Labor.

Distribution of human population from Internal Labor Process to External Labor Process

Our characterization of the two aspects of human labor indicates their essentially complementary nature. Each one depends upon the other if it is to operate for any length of time. Each produces the specific earth materials which the other uses as an integral part of its activities. At the same time, neither produces the materials which it uses. The unity of Internal Labor and External Labor is therefore a necessary condition for the effective operation of either one singly, or of both together. This implies the existence of a set of social mechanisms to forge that unity.

The unity must take place in two ways. One set of institutions must provide for transferring food from the External Labor Process, where it is created, to the Internal Labor Process, where it is used. Another set of institutions must provide for transferring people from the Internal Labor Process, where they are created, to the External Labor Process, where they are used. We shall refer to these institutional mechanisms as Distribution Processes.

In order that people will in fact leave the Internal Labor Process for the External Labor Process, it is convenient to postulate the existence of a set of forces in the latter process which operates with effective impact to attract the requisite number of people. A little reflection will convince us that such a force is inherent in the number of people actually performing External Labor.

We must recall that External Labor cannot begin without a certain number of people already on hand. As the labor activity proceeds, the laboring people are simultaneously being used up. As a matter of fact, we can measure the inherent period in the cycle of External Labor by the interval of time it takes for the initial stock of people to reduce down to zero. The attractive force of the External Labor Process can therefore be assumed to be inversely proportional to the number of people generating External Labor at a given point in time. Put another way, the magnitude of the attractive force of External Labor upon the people in the Internal Labor Process is directly proportional to the time expired in the cycle of External Labor. This is a necessary condition for maintaining the level and continuity of External Labor.

At the same time, the level of resistance of the people within the Internal Labor Process to the attractions of External Labor must be sufficiently weak so as to be overcome. We shall argue that the extent of the resistance within the Internal Labor Process is directly proportional to the quantity of food within the Internal Labor Process.

We may recall that the Internal Labor Process cannot begin unless there is already on hand a certain stock of food. The inherent period in the cycle of Internal Labor is measured by the interval of time it takes for the initial stock of food to reduce down to zero. In other words, the magnitude of the resistance of the people within the Internal Labor Process to the forces of attraction from the External Labor Process is indirectly proportional to the time expired in the cycle of Internal Labor. That is to say, resistance is greatest at the start of the cycle of Internal Labor, when the initial stock of food is untouched; resistance is totally collapsed at the end of the Internal Labor period, when the initial stock of food has been completely used up.

To describe these events in terms of attractive forces and resisting forces gives an air of mechanical unreality to the underlying dynamics of what is actually taking place. The general character of these forces is manifested in the concept of "property." This concept gives rise at once to the notion that people must be categorized in at least two distinct roles – those who own the Internal Labor Process and those who own the External Labor Process.

The general nature of political economy

Forces of attraction and repulsion are then nothing more than special forms in which human will is exercised in the transfer of people from the Internal Labor Process to the External Labor Process. It is indeed the people who own the External Labor Process who actively seek out and otherwise induce, coerce, cajole, and entice people to enter on External Labor. Similarly, it is the people who own the Internal Labor Process who must consciously acquiesce to their opposite colleagues and thereby actually provide the requisite number of live bodies required by the External Labor Process.

On a more fundamental level, the Process of Distribution of the people from the Internal Labor Process to the External Labor Process is the social mechanism which provides for the ceding of property in the human person by those who own the Internal Labor Process. At the same time, it is also the acquisition of proprietorship over human persons by those who own the External Labor Process. The same property – a certain number of people, who have been ceded by one group – is acquired by another group. In a dialectical sense, property rights in the people have been abrogated; simultaneously, property rights in the people have been reinstituted. This is the fundamental role of the Process of Distribution of people from the Internal Labor Process to the External Labor Process.

Distribution of food from External Labor Process to Internal Labor Process

We now know that the other link in joining the two labor processes together is a social mechanism which transfers food from the External Labor Process, in which it is created, to the Internal Labor Process, in which it is used. We shall postulate the existence of a set of forces in the latter process which operates to attract the requisite quantity of food. We also assume that such a force is inherent in the quantity of food actually being consumed in the Internal Labor Process.

As Internal Labor proceeds, the initial stock of food which it must have on hand to start the operations is simultaneously being used up. A measure of the inherent period in the cycle of Internal Labor is the interval of time it takes for the initial stock of food to reduce down to zero. The attractive force of Internal Labor can therefore be assumed to be inversely proportional to the quantity of food effectively undergoing Internal Labor at a given moment in time. Put another way, the attractive force is directly proportional to the time expired in the cycle of Internal Labor. This is a necessary condition for maintaining the level and continuity of Internal Labor.

At the same time, the level of resistance of the food within the External Labor Process to the attractions of Internal Labor must be sufficiently weakened so as to be overcome. We shall argue that the extent of the resistance within the External Labor Process is directly proportional to the number of people performing External Labor.

We must recall that External Labor cannot begin unless there is on hand a certain initial number of people. The inherent period within which such labor takes place is measured by the interval of time it takes for the initial stock of people to reduce down to zero. In other words, the magnitude of the resistance of food within the External Labor Process to the forces of attraction of the Internal Labor Process is indirectly proportional to the time expired in the cycle of External Labor. That is to say, resistance is greatest at the start of the cycle of External Labor, when the initial number of people is untouched; resistance totally collapses at the end of the cycle of External Labor, when the initial number of people has been totally used up.

These attracting and resisting forces are manifestations of two categories of people consciously interacting under property relationships. It is the people who own the Internal Labor Process who consciously offer the inducements to get possession of the food supply. At the same time, it is the people who own the External Labor Process whose resistance must be overcome. What we have here is fundamentally the institutional norms under which those who own the External Labor Process cede their property rights in food. At the same time, those who own the Internal Labor Process acquire property rights in food.

The terms of the cession and acquisition of property are such that the underlying forces of attraction and resistance must be equal in some sense. This must be so inasmuch as it is precisely the same food which has been ceded by one group of people and acquired by another group. We also have here the dialectical

The general nature of political economy

process of abrogation of property rights in food; simultaneously, property rights in the same food have been reinstituted. This is the fundamental role of the Process of Distribution of food from the External Labor Process to the Internal Labor Process.

The two distribution processes, functioning simultaneously, lay the basis for the unity of the two labor processes. As such, most of the conditions for the perpetual generation of labor are in hand. However, the conditions established thus far tell us how the labor processes can carry out, in ever recurring cycles, a set of activities at some pre-established level and intensity. Nothing has been said about the possibility of moving beyond the levels of the initial cycle.

At the end of each cycle of labor, certain results ensue. A certain number of people has been produced in the Internal Labor Process; at the same time another number of people has been used up in the External Labor Process. Similarly, a certain quantity of food has been produced in the External Labor Process; at the same time another quantity of food has been used up in the Internal Labor Process. As a consequence, there is some "excess" (positive, negative, or zero) of people and food over and beyond their initial levels. These excesses, in conjunction with their initial stocks, must be put back into the same relationships which define the mechanisms of social reproduction within the political economy.

The specific quantities of these "excesses," and the peculiar way in which they are recombined to reproduce the defining characteristics of the political economy are the roles of the Process of Accumulation of Wealth.

Process of Accumulation of Wealth

The fact that wealth pervades all manner of human society gives it a sort of intuitive understanding by practically everyone. Its presence is highly visible in the ostentatious display of ownership and consumption of material goods by those whom we think of as being wealthy. In contrast, the miserable and depraved conditions of those who are without it manifest its opposite in poverty. Thus, every schoolchild knows at once who is wealthy and who is poor. By inference, wealth comes to be known by its visible effects.

Yet, a general definition of wealth is quite missing from the literature of political economy. It is usually associated with non-human earth materials – money, houses, factories, silks, precious metals, animal herds, stores of consumables, etc. On occasion, it is associated with persons in the form of slaves.

We shall postulate in this work that wealth is in essence "the material synthesis of the human population and its food supply, bound together in a combined producing and consuming mode, in such a way as to preserve the characteristics of the political economy in which it is created."

It is a "social" concept, inasmuch as its function is indelibly tied to the very nature of the political economy. It is the key variable in defining the rules of the game.

At this stage of generality we cannot specify the exact form of the synthesis. Nevertheless, the possibilities are limited in types, if not in variety of actual forms. Since it is a synthesis of the human population and its food supply, the general form the synthesis takes has to be a combination of its elements – human population and food. Now, there are four general forms possible on the basis of such a combination – (a) a simple collection of the human population and its food supply, (b) the human population only, (c) the food supply only, and (d) a combination of the human population and the food supply in a form that is distinct from any of the two elements – human population, food – of the synthesis.

The last form mentioned above is quite interesting. It has the potential for distinguishing a wide variety of sub-forms. Four such sub-forms are readily identified – (1) both human-like and food-like, (2) human-like only, (3) food-like only, (4) neither human-like nor food-like. We have apparently opened up a Pandora's box. Nevertheless, once we recall that there is one dominant form that defines the characteristics of the political economy, the problem becomes more manageable.

The "synthesis" may be conceived of as a quantitative concept, inasmuch as "quantities" of the elements enter into its definition. On the other hand, the synthesis is a qualitative concept, inasmuch as it has a specific material form. We shall postulate in this work that the qualitative aspect – the specific form it assumes – is strictly a function of the ratio of the quantities of the elements which go to make it up. In other words, it is the long-term stable quantitative relationship between the human population and its food supply which defines the form of wealth in the political economy.

The general nature of political economy

The quantitative magnitude of the elements of wealth springs from the resulting effects of the two labor processes and the two distribution processes.

Internal and External Labor, once joined, are two different phases of the same activity. One phase is internally directed onto the human population itself; the other phase is directed outside of the human population onto the earth. The single labor activity manifested in two opposing, but complementary, phases – Internal and External – is indeed the pulsating heartbeat of the human population in its continuous quest for survival. External Labor produces the non-human material means of the people's survival. Internal Labor uses these materials to create the people. Both phases of the laboring activity are generated by the same human population. The common, but alternating, magnitude of each labor phase is the effort required to burst asunder the shackles of property relations which bind the people to their food supply.

The two Distribution Processes operate as a unity to bind the people to their food supply in a specific way. One process dictates the conditions under which they may have the opportunity to produce their food supply; the other process dictates the quantity of food the people may receive for their personal consumption. The binding force represented by the unity of these two distribution processes is an indication of the form of property relations endemic to the system of political economy. It is precisely this force which the two labor processes attempt to destroy, because they establish impediments to the people's ability to freely produce and consume their food supply.

The quantity of food produced is a measure of the quantity of input of the External Labor Process. The quantity of food distributed to the Internal Labor Process is a measure of the output of the External Labor Process. The difference between the two is potentially the gross accumulation of External Labor in the form of food.

Similarly, the quantity of the population produced is a measure of input of the Internal Labor Process. The number of people distributed to the External Labor Process is a measure of the output of the Internal Labor Process. The difference between the two is potentially the gross accumulation of Internal Labor in the form of people.

Wealth Accumulation, first and foremost, requires the actual success in generating gross accumulations of Internal and External Labor. Secondly, and of signal importance, a certain portion of the accumulated Internal Labor must be joined with a certain portion of accumulated External Labor in the precise way in which the initial stocks of food and people were distributed to their respective labor processes. This second act is the reproduction of the two distribution processes. Thus, the conditions for reproduction of the two labor processes are set. In this way, the Accumulation of Wealth insures the continuity of the same type of political economy into the future.

It must be emphasized that Wealth Accumulation is not done in the abstract. Indeed, it must be carried out by the exercise of the conscious will of people acting in the role of wealth accumulators. These wealth owners have the onus of preserving the form of their wealth while, at the same time, striving to increase its magnitude. Just as important, is the necessity for continuous control over the Wealth Accumulation Process by the wealth owners. Hence, the wealth relationships manifested in the operation of the two labor processes and the two distribution processes must be ever repeated again and again for prolonged periods of time, in such a way that the form of wealth is preserved and the wealth owners are reproduced as wealth owners.

The Wealth Accumulation Process is the creative activity which reproduces the system of political economy. But the system *qua* system has to be managed. The rules of the game must be abided by. And the power to monitor the behavior of the active agents and to enforce the rules of distribution, labor, and wealth accumulation must reside in some institution within the system of political economy. Indeed, such an institution is the Political State.

The Political State

The Political State is a very important institution which operates in all political economies. It is the institution charged with the function of establishing and enforcing the rules of operation of the political economy. Its power is absolute over all the human members of the population. It garners unto itself a monopoly of force and violence to be used as its own dictates demand.

As an institution it must function in compliance with the will of

The general nature of political economy

human agents. Its primary function is to protect the property rights of members of the population in the ownership of the material elements of the society. Thus, it must issue rules which legitimize the operations of the two labor processes, the two distribution processes, and the wealth accumulating process.

To carry out its mission it must organize and use resources, both people as well as food. But it must function within the very rules it establishes, while at the same time standing above these rules as final arbiter in matters under dispute. It is easy to infer that the organizational apparatus (government bureaucracy) through which it functions will simulate the activities of the two labor processes, the two distribution processes, and the wealth accumulating process.

Since it is the main instrument for insuring the continued reproduction of wealth in its characteristic form, it may be viewed as wealth personified. Put another way, those who control this institution, as distinct from those who function within it, are the personifications of wealth. The state, therefore, may be viewed as the institution which impresses the binding force upon the system. It is the synthesizing agent which keeps the two labor processes joined together in opposing, but complementary, roles. It thus insures that the system functions as a living organism. The extent of the binding force is to be sought in the enforcement of the rules of distribution.

The specific character of the state and the degree of complexity with which it organizes an apparatus (government bureaucracy) to carry out its mission are both determined by the specific type of society over which it presides.

The outside world

It is not enough to peek inside a given political economy in isolation from the world context in which it functions. It certainly influences the outcomes of world events and, in turn, is influenced by the geographic domains outside its own borders. The extent of these joint influences depends upon the degree to which the political economy in question is in active contacts with its outside neighbors.

Peaceable interactions through trade or cultural exchanges may characterize the nature of the outside influences. On the other hand, there may be warlike intercourse such as conquest, colonization, enslavement, economic imperialism, etc., which are also possible. In any event, any or all of these connections will have a decisive effect on the operations and outcomes of the political economy.

Finally, there remains the possibility that one or a few outside political economies monopolize the overwhelming part of the earth's surface as their peculiar geographic domain. This means that the space available to the economy in question becomes somewhat restricted. Furthermore, the impacts of the outside economies on the oxygen in the atmosphere, on the quantity of sunlight reaching the earth's surface, on the quantity and quality of rainfall, on the purity of the ocean fisheries, etc. could be devastating.

The concept of time in political economies

All political economies are suffused with human labor. As an activity, labor takes place over an interval of time; it has a specific duration. But human labor has two forms, two essentially connected phases – Internal and External. The unified operation of these two sequentially connected phases of the same activity implies an inherent labor period. Within such a period both phases of labor, both distribution processes which unite them, and the Wealth Accumulation Process which restarts the cycle of reproduction are all consummated at some standard quantum of operations. The notion of time as a repetitive cycle of labor is the concept which corresponds to this type of event. This is the notion of "periodic time."

Once the cycle of reproduction is started, another concept of time emerges. This is the passage of days, or years, or decades, or centuries during which the nature of the social reproductive process undergoes no qualitative change, although it may undergo quantitative change. During such an interval of time the people are reproduced as the same genre from which they sprang at the beginning of the interval; the institutions of social reproduction function precisely the same way throughout the interval; and the political state maintains its basic characteristics. These events define the concept of "historical time."

Still another concept of time is associated with the clock or calendar, in so far as it is commonly designated and recognized by

The general nature of political economy

people in all geographical domains of the earth. This is the concept of "real time." It is indeed the barometer of correspondence between events in a particular political economy and all the others outside its geographic area.

Real time is obviously the most general concept. Historical time is applicable to all people in every geographic domain experiencing the same type of political economy. Periodic time is applicable to one human population within a given geographic domain. What is important in making these distinctions is that at a particular moment in real time, people in different geographic domains may be undergoing quite different historical epochs. It is also possible that people in different geographic domains who are experiencing the same historical epoch may have quite different periodic times in the generation of their labor.

As cases in point, on May 1, 1982 the United States and the Soviet Union were undergoing different historical epochs; the former was in a capitalist era, while the latter was in a socialist era. Similarly, on that date the two geographically distinct peoples of Great Britain and of Japan were both existing in a capitalist epoch, but were apparently subject to different periodicities in their labor cycles. The Japanese would seem to have a more quickened pace in the completion of the two phases of their labor cycle.

These temporal distinctions will prove to be rather important when we try to observe events in the real world. In any case, they should be appreciated when studying the black condition in the United States. They will help us to unravel what appears to be an otherwise complex pattern of economic development of these blacks as they traversed the ocean sea and survived within the bowels of the larger United States political economies as a distinctive people under the historical epochs of slavery, sharecropping, and wage laboring.

Political economies in the real world

The description which we have thus far given of the general nature of political economy is just that – very general indeed. Nowhere in the world today, nor in the past, can one empirically identify a political economy which exhibits these descriptive features in an obvious way. The reason for this is quite simple; principles of

The general nature of political economy

political economy are actually played out in the real world under a wide variety of influences on specific peoples, within many locations on the face of the earth, under very different types of institutions, and at distinctive eras of historical development.

These influences give rise to the concept of special types of political economy. Each such special type conforms to the general description; however, each type carries out its reproductive functions in ways which are peculiar to it. The essential meaning of all this is that we cannot escape empirical observations if we are to understand the general case. We must confront reality through deliberate study of the vast number of actual political economies which have functioned on the face of the earth from the beginnings of the human condition.

In the following chapter we turn to a consideration of the special types of political economies.

2 Special types of political economies

The general model of political economy postulated in Chapter 1 lends itself to a wide range of special applications in the real world. That model generalized political economy in terms of six basic factors. Indeed, the general nature of political economy stemmed from the fact that we did not specify any magnitude nor form of any of the six factors.

Analytically, these six factors constitute a set of constraining parameters which gives the political economy its special characteristics. Each distinct combination of these six parameters defines a "special" political economy. Once we admit that in the real world it is possible for each of these six parameters to have hundreds of different forms, then for all practical purposes the number of special political economies is unlimited.

On the face of the earth today there are hundreds of geographical domains which can be differentiated from each other by their national boundaries. A few countries – the United States, Canada, Soviet Union, People's Republic of China – occupy vast physical areas. On the other hand, many countries – El Salvador, Barbados, Belize – are of insignificant size. The rest of the countries fall everywhere along the size continuum between these two extreme groups. In addition to size, the various countries are blessed with different conditions of climate, weather patterns, physical topography, ocean access, rivers, mountains, forests, topsoil, potable water, plants, animals, minerals.

The people being reproduced in the various countries exhibit wide differences in physical and social traits. They come in all sizes – from an average of four feet or so to over seven feet tall. Their skins are stamped with every conceivable color. Their age distribu-

Special types of political economies

tions vary in a continuum from a concentration in the very young ages to a concentration in the elderly group. They practice a number of different religions – Christianity, Judaism, Hinduism, Islam. They operate from day to day as integral members of families, or clans, or tribes, or classes, or castes, or ethnic groups, or nationalities.

The institutional mechanisms of social reproduction differ markedly from one people to the next. Distributions may be accomplished by means of buying and selling, or by barter, or by gift, or by fiat. External and Internal Labor may be generated under complete coercion of one group by an outside group, or by voluntary acquiescence to the will of the outside group, or by mutual agreement among peers of the same group. Accumulation of wealth may be realized by amassing stocks of money, or food, or slaves, or cowries.

The different historical epochs in which the people are currently being reproduced are reflected in the popular names – communism, socialism, capitalism, slavery, feudalism, tribalism, communalism – given to the social orders which prevail.

The essential characteristics of the political state also differ among the various countries. North Americans like to think of their political state as the paragon of democracy. On the other hand, they speak of the brutality of Soviet tyranny. They also characterize many of the Third World political states as being run by military dictatorships or by civilian native elite groups who rule for selfish purposes or for tribal ascendancy.

Finally, the state of the outside world differs from country to country. For example, the huge giants like the United States or the Soviet Union can obviously dictate to the smaller and weaker countries; correspondingly, the tiny countries like Barbados and El Salvador are passive reactors to events in the outside world.

Historical and dialectical materialism

The serious student of political economy must find this situation to be agonizingly disappointing. Empirical study of the limitless number of possible special cases will surely boggle the mind. But don't be alarmed. There is a way out of this morass. It was precisely

Special types of political economies

the attempt to classify the various specialized systems of political economy that led to a most amazing discovery in the social sciences.

Karl Marx is to be given the lion's share of credit for inventing the theory generally referred to as historical and dialectical materialism. This theory acknowledges that there could conceivably exist millions of distinct types of political economies; however, it hypothesizes that the real world is much more restricted than the conceptual possibilities. Only a small number of distinct types of political economies has been actually observed. Apparently the six parameters are not independent of each other; there must be a tight web of interdependence linking them together.

Marx claimed to have identified only four types of human social organizations in existence or to have existed during his day. He labeled these societies as communalism, slavery, feudalism, and capitalism. The theory was created out of his attempt to understand the nature of capitalist society. He demonstrated that capitalist society as it existed in Great Britain during the middle of the nineteenth century was a relatively new system of political economy. It originated out of the conditions which made for the destruction of the feudal society which preceded it.

He dated the origin of British capitalism at the Glorious Revolution of the late seventeenth century, which established the hegemony of the capitalist class over the national political state in triumph over the landed aristocracy who had dominated the feudal era. He found the preconditions for capitalism to have begun to take root from about the middle of the sixteenth century inside the bowels of the feudal society.

The preconditions for the establishment of the capitalist society were said to be the coming into being of a class of capitalists and a class of wage laborers. The former was a group of people who privately owned a mass of accumulated capital; the latter was a group of people who were divorced from their means of subsistence and their means of production and owned nothing but their ability to work. Some of the specific events which brought these two classes into existence were

> The spoliation of the church's property, the fraudulent alienation of the State domains, the robbery of the common lands, the usurpation of feudal and clan property, and its transformation into modern private property under

circumstances of reckless terrorism, were just so many idyllic methods of primitive accumulation. They conquered the field for capitalistic agriculture, made the soil part and parcel of capital, and created for the town industries the necessary supply of a "free" and outlawed proletariat.

Once the connection is made between capitalism and feudalism, the question of the origin of feudalism surfaces. The Marxian analysis demonstrated that feudalism originated out of the dissolution of the slave societies which functioned under the Roman Empire. Finally, it was argued that slavery originated out of the breakdown of communal society.

The theory, then, not only postulates the four types of political economies; it also postulates that any given human society evolves through these four types in one and only one sequence — from communalism, to slavery, to feudalism to capitalism. Moreover, capitalism is not an eternal system; it has a birth date, it develops, and it will surely die. The future outcome of the dissolution of capitalism was predicted by Marx to be a system of political economy called socialism.

This is heady stuff. As historical hypothesis it can be subjected to empirical refutation. In any case, it serves a most useful function in enabling the student to classify the apparently unlimited forms of human social organization which presently exist in the world. But it does much more; it makes possible a way of marshalling relevant facts to illuminate the historical development and future outcome of any given people.

Black Americans, as a distinct people, may certainly be analyzed in terms of the Marxian hypothesis. They have been at one time in their history slaves; at another time they have been landless peasants working under conditions akin to feudalism in the southern sharecropping system; and they are now integral members of the wage working class under the American capitalist system. It is also well known that at some time in their history on the African continent they existed in communal settings. Perhaps we may at least get the opportunity to test out the implications of historical and dialectical materialism from an appropriate study of the black experience in the United States.

An important aspect of the Marxian hypothesis is the dialectical principle. It argues that each type of political economy contains an inherent contradiction. This contradiction is also precisely the motor which drives the system and makes it grow quantitatively. But at some decisive moment in history the contradiction explodes into a general crisis; the system of political economy is rent asunder; a new system of political economy is born out of the old.

In summary, the theory postulates a one-to-one correspondence between (a) the defining characteristics of a human population, residing in a particular country, at a given moment in real time; and (b) the method by which the institutions of social reproduction effectively function, under the rule of the political state. This method – the unified and interdependent link-up of labor, distribution, and accumulation under the rules enforced by the political state – designates a specific historical epoch.

The historical epoch, in turn, is labeled communalism, or slavery, or feudalism, or capitalism, or socialism. Progression of a people from one historical epoch to another is postulated to follow the ordered sequence in which we have listed the labels above. Furthermore, this is the only sequence possible.

It necessarily follows that if one observes a particular human population, in a specific country, over a sufficiently long period of real time, it is possible that one would behold a panorama of all five historical epochs, following one upon another in the postulated sequence. As the people moved from one historical epoch to another, the observer would see them undergo a revolutionary change in their defining characteristics at some particular moment. Yet, the keen observer would have noticed that the preconditions for such a radical break with the past were long gestating in the previous epoch and were indeed integral aspects of that past epoch. This is the meaning of the dialectical principle.

It necessarily follows that at any given moment in real time throughout the world we will actually observe every one of the five historical epochs, occurring among different groups of people, located in different countries. We will also observe a number of these people in transition – evolving – from one epoch to another. And to further complicate matters, different people in the same historical epoch will be observed to exhibit peculiarly national differences in their ways of carrying out the same type of social reproduction. As if this isn't sufficiently complicated, within some particular country we will also observe more than one distinctive

Special types of political economies

people simultaneously undergoing social reproduction, with each such people subject to a different historical epoch.

This rich variety of reality – this apparently complex empirical syndrome, this diversity among the various peoples in countries throughout the world – is simply an indication of the different stages of development of the various people, the different historical epochs of their social reproduction, each proceeding apace at the very same moment in real time. But in this diversity is the underlying unity in the sense that each population group has undergone or is undergoing the same five epochs in its development and in exactly the same sequence.

In the application of these principles to blacks we should be able to identify the specific moment in time when they ceased to be communal people and became slaves; when they ceased to be slaves and became landless peasants; and when they ceased to be landless peasants and became wage laborers. However, we must also diligently seek to identify the development of the preconditions for these abrupt changes during the fifty or even one hundred years before they occurred. For example, in the great migrations of blacks from the southern lands to the cities of the country at large, over a period of more than fifty years, we witness one of the mechanisms which operated to evolve them from their sharecropping status to a bona fide wage laboring class.

In what follows we shall detail the essential description of each of the five historical epochs. In each case we shall rely on the principle that the decisive distinction between the different types of political economies – the different historical epochs – is to be found in the qualitative form of the most important materials of wealth which prevail.

We shall rely on the principle that the basic contradiction of the system indeed resides within the very structure of wealth itself. As synthesis of the human population and the food made available for its personal consumption, the extent of the binding force is to be measured by the pressures exerted by the wealth owners, buttressed by the Political State, through the instrumentality of the distribution processes, legitimately to rivet the workers to a particular mode of exploitation.

The extent of this binding force must be matched by two oppositely directed analytic forces – the acts of Internal and External Labor. The greater the binding force, the greater must be the

Special types of political economies

intensity of labor. In time, the binding force is torn asunder; the working people are liberated from the shackles of the characteristic modes of distribution. A new historical epoch is born, with its attendant characteristic forms of labor, distribution, and wealth accumulation.

Communal society

The communal society is one in which wealth is a simple collection of the human population and its food supply.

The distribution of the human population to the External Labor Process is based on the mutually agreed upon decisions by the people to assign and accept equal tasks.

The distribution of the food supply to the Internal Labor Process is accomplished on the basis of similar mutually agreed upon decisions to share equally in the fruits of their External Labor.

Internal Labor is implemented through the agency of the extended family. Food is consumed as communal property. The children issuing from birth are the common wards of the entire population.

In this historical epoch there is no wealth accumulation. The synthesizing forces of the distribution processes are in perfect harmony with the analytic forces of the two labor processes. Indeed, the human population is in dynamic harmony with the earth.

We are dealing here with societies which dominated the earth in the era of hunters and fishers and gatherers. It is Adam Smith's "original state of things, which precedes both the appropriation of land and the accumulation of stock" and "in which the whole produce of labour belongs to the labourer. He has neither landlord nor master to share with him." Some such societies still exist on the face of the earth today. The Tassaday people of the Philippines, the Pygmies of Africa, some tribes of the Amazon rain forests are examples of communal epochs.

There is no inherent contradiction in such a society. It remains stable throughout the years, perhaps changing only in response to the vagaries of the earth in its own general geologic traumas, or in the accidents to which all humans are prone from time to time. Under these circumstances the only general crisis which may befall this society to transform it into another type must come from human agents outside its geographic domain.

It is an alien people, imposing its will on the tranquil domestic order, that will disturb the peaceful and harmonious coexistence of the communal population and its earth mother. Indeed, it is the successful wielding of superior force in the clash of arms that gives the victorious alien invaders the opportunity to expropriate the natives as private property. Henceforth, the conditions are set for conquest and stealth of communal people as private property of others, until the social order is dominated by a class of slave masters and a class of slaves. The death knell sounds for communalism; slavery is born out of the demise.

Slave society

The slave society is one in which wealth has the form of people, owned by another group of people. There are thus two classes of people – masters and slaves – within the population. Masters are distinguished as owners of wealth in slaves. Slaves are private property of the masters. This is the first historical epoch in which the population becomes fractionated into a ruling class and a working class.

The distribution of slaves from the Internal Labor Process to the External Labor Process is strictly determined and enforced by the personal dictates of the slave master. Similarly, the distribution of food from the External Labor Process to the Internal Labor Process is exclusively determined by the iron will of the slave master.

The Internal Labor Process is under the complete personal ownership and control of the slave master. He personally dictates the types and quantities of human slaves to be created out of the given food rations. In addition, it is the slave master who likewise dictates the degree of intensity of Internal Labor which is to be performed by the slave.

The External Labor Process is likewise under the complete ownership and control of the slave master. He personally dictates the quantity of food to be produced as well as the quantity of other non-human earth materials, if any. It is obvious that the slave master also dictates the degree of intensity of External Labor which is extracted from the slave.

Special types of political economies

Wealth Accumulation must reproduce the slave relations. An essential condition to be satisfied is that the human population must be reproduced as a slave population. Correspondingly, the net reproduction of food must be the private property of the slave master. Finally, the synthesis of the net reproduction of the slave population and the net reproduction of the food supply must take on the form of living human slaves. In practical terms, this translates into the condition that the final form of wealth in the epoch of slavery must be such that the quantity of slaves vastly exceeds the quantity of food made available to them for their own personal consumption.

In contrast to the communal society, the slave is rather scantily supplied with the means of survival. At the same time, we can expect these means of survival to be of the minimal type required for the reproduction of the slave. Food in minimal quantities, but highly concentrated in calories, is what the slave is provided with. If anything else is provided it must be only the by-products of the food itself.

This implies that in slave society the intensification of Internal Labor is absolute, to the limits of the capacity of the slaves. This must be so in order that the scant supplies of food may effectively reproduce the required number of slave babies.

The External Labor of the slave can also be assumed to be pushed to the limits of the slaves' capacities. The slaves must not only produce food for their own reproduction, but must produce much more to satisfy the food requirements of the slave master. In addition the slaves must produce other non-human earth materials for the personal consumption and ostentatious display of the slave master.

A very important fact is not well understood by most scholars who have analyzed slave societies. All of the non-human earth materials produced by the slaves in the External Labor Process are completely free of "cost" to the slave master. Therefore, there can be no calculation of "profit" in the epoch of slavery. The absence of costs means that profit cannot be defined. "Revenue" in the form of the results of the External Labor Process is the crucial factor. Hence, the relevant behavior of the slave master meets with no impediments to pushing for maximum production of his own food supply as well as of the other "luxury" items necessary to maintain his stature and power.

Special types of political economies

Since wealth is accumulated privately, the total wealth of the slave society is a simple summation of the wealth of each slave master within the geographical domain. The Political State enforces its rules through the individual slave master's personal use of force, together with other social institutions agreed upon and established by these same masters. It is obvious that the extent of power within the Political State will vary among slave masters in direct proportion to their wealth holdings in the form of slaves.

Slave societies have existed in many countries throughout history. Black slavery in the United States is an important case in point. But slavery was also extensive throughout the ancient Greek and Roman Empires. It was rampant in the Arab world even centuries before the Atlantic slave trade by the Western Europeans. Today it is said to be outlawed in all countries. However, from time to time instances of slavery surface in the news reports.

The major contradiction which inheres in slave society must be sought in the very nature of the characteristic form of wealth. The binding force which rivets the slave population to its food supply is the personal pressures exerted by the masters upon the backs of the slaves. At the same time, however, the pulsating heartbeats of the slaves' labors, alternately Internal and External, represent the struggle to break out of bondage. This struggle continues unabatedly, sometimes erupting in dramatic acts of individual revolt or rebellion; but in an indirect way the counter forces exerted by the slave can be measured by the extent of visible applications of repressive deeds by the slave masters in their day to day rounds. The continual presence of weapons carried by the masters and their overseers; the total social, educational, political, religious, and other restrictions placed upon the slaves from sun-up to sundown; the ever debauching of slave womanhood – are manifestations of the measure of slave rebellion against the conditions of servitude.

At some point in time this contradiction erupts to free the slaves from the shackles that bind them to a slave mode of existence within the bowels of the slave owner's private property. This result can be accelerated by outside forces; but more important are the forces stemming from the slaves' labors in all their ramifications. At the time of death, the slave society will have achieved its highest capabilities (looked at from the standpoint of the slave masters), but its demise will bring into being the birthing of the feudal epoch.

Special types of political economies

In the case of the United States, the demise of slavery was finally consummated by the successful military conquest of the slaveocrats by northern capitalists, who deliberately sought control of the national state power. The Roman Empire disintegrated under the onslaught of the so-called barbarians who swarmed over the outer fringes of the imperial domains. This is not to belittle, however, the internal contradictions of the slave society which were continuously ground out for a great number of years before the demise.

In any case, a critical consequence of the demise of slavery is the "freeing" of the slaves. This decisive act destroys slave master wealth, because it destroys the basis of that wealth. But it also frees up the slaves' food supply. The new ruling class in the succeeding feudal order will therefore be the human agents who spread out their safety nets to capture ownership and control of the former slaves' food supply. This will become their basis of power and control over the feudal working class.

Feudal society

In feudal society wealth has the characteristic form of food. Two types of people characterize this society. Landlords privately own the food supply; landless peasants own nothing but themselves. Thus, feudal society is the second historical epoch in the lives of a people in which they are divided into distinctive economic classes.

The distribution of peasants from the Internal Labor Process to the External Labor Process is accomplished through the instrumentality of a formal agreement, a contract, hammered out between a landlord and one or more peasants. Under the uneven circumstances which characterize the relationship, we may assume that the "hungry" peasant doesn't have much of an alternative in the matter.

The quantity of food distributed from the External Labor Process to the Internal Labor Process is based on the same contractual arrangement which brings the peasant to the External Labor Process.

In this historical epoch the two distribution processes are indistinguishable one from another. They operate as a unity at all times to provide peasant fodder to the External Labor Process, on the one hand, and to supply to the peasant the food for her/his survival, on the other hand. On a general level, the unity of these two processes represents a conversion of the existing peasant population into the food made available for personal consumption by that same population, and conversely.

The "agreement" or contract between the landlord and the peasant which makes the conversion possible yields up to the peasant a certain percentage of the food produced by the peasant; the remainder goes to the landlord. This is the concept of "sharecropping"; that is, remuneration is paid in kind to the peasant, in the form of the very type of materials produced by that peasant. This contrasts with money wage payments.

Whatever the amount of the compensation in kind, arrived at on the basis of the share agreement, we can assume that on a national level it must be at least sufficient to reproduce the peasant population. A certain minimal quantity of food must constitute part of this payment in kind; other non-food materials received will depend upon special circumstances within the domestic economy and its relation to the outside world.

For example, when the system of black sharecropping prevailed in the southern United States the immediate produce of the cropper was generally in the form of cotton, a non-human earth material that is not capable of personal consumption by the cropper. In any event, because of the existence in the "outside" world of merchants who readily exchanged the cotton for food supplies, both the cropper and the landlord could easily convert their respective shares of cotton into food. On the contrary, at some moments in real time during the feudal epoch in Western Europe, the isolation of some manors from outside contacts precluded such happenings. Hence, the immediate produce of the peasants had to be food.

We do not have in hand any ready-made principle with which to gauge the relevant proportions in which the production of food by the peasant is shared with the landlord. Yet, it may not be too far-fetched to assume that such sharing agreements will always yield up to the peasant less than fifty per cent of the crop she/he produces. Fifty per cent implies equal sharing and therefore equal powers of the parties to the contract. We should think that landlords have had the upper hand, and that as the ruling class, must usurp the position of power over the peasant. Hence, we should expect to observe in the real world agreements which set the share of the peasant somewhat below the fifty per cent standard.

Special types of political economies

In typical cases of black sharecropping in the southern United States fifty per cent sharing was written into the documents. However, by hook and crook, landlords were able to extract significant portions of the black cropper's so-called half share, so that debt peonage became more than just a passing phenomenon. Indeed, the typical cropper could be said to have been able merely to subsist on his meager food rations. Beyond that he might end up, at best, without indebtedness to the landlord or to the merchant; or, at worst, he would end up in perpetual and increasing debt.

In this epoch the External Labor Process is under the complete control of the landlord. It is he who dictates what is to be produced and in what quantities. Because of the percentage share arrangement, however, the intensity of External Labor can be left to the peasant's discretion. After all, if the amount of food made available through the share agreement is kept at minimum, then the peasant has all the incentive in the world to produce more than heretofore. At an unchanging percentage share, greater production means greater absolute sharing.

The Internal Labor Process is the private domain of the peasant family. The technology developed in this process must be such that the peasant family survives. With a paucity of food to be consumed, the Internal Labor Process must extend to the limits of the capacity of the peasant family in order that the basis of a continuing population of peasants can be laid down. In other words, the intensity of Internal Labor must generate a relatively large number of annual births as a peasant characteristic. Such intensity of labor, while carried out by the will of the peasant, is nevertheless a necessary consequence of the share arrangements which obviously favored the landlord's interests. In short, the free peasant has few degrees of freedom in determining the intensity of his Internal Labor efforts.

The Process of Accumulation of Wealth must insure the reproduction of the feudal relations. This implies that the net reproduction of the peasant population and the net reproduction of the food supply must be synthesized as food, privately owned by the landlord. Simultaneously, the surviving peasant population must be free, but without any private stocks of food.

This condition can be achieved if the peasants are in such a position that it is impossible to accumulate any non-human survival materials, including food; and if the landlords are in a position to use the net reproduction of food for their own personal consumption as well as to use some to employ the peasantry in the production of non-food "luxuries" for the landlords' own personal aggrandizement. These latter may be fancy mansions, dapper clothing, household fineries, exotic merchandise from foreign lands, monuments, and other ostentatious displays of power and prestige and social dominance.

The feudal Political State must enforce the rules of formation of landlord private property. The state and its complementary prevailing institutions will therefore enforce the rights of the landlords to extort a portion of the peasant's labors, free of charge, by virtue of their class position. At the same time, however, it is the very possibility of the availability of non-food materials to the landlords on the basis of the feudal relations which tolls the bells of doom for the system.

The more successful the landlords in the accumulation of feudal private property, the greater is the amount of non-food materials which they are able to command. Whether or not these are produced domestically, they are omens of a new element, requiring for its production a more roundabout process. And the method of procuring such an element may require new forms of distribution. If they are acquired outside the feudal geographical domain it may well entail buying and selling arrangements, with intermediaries such as merchants, traders, and the like. But sooner or later the social relations stimulated and encouraged by the landlords' consumption of non-food material means of survival intensify the contradictions which undermine the system's foundations and ultimately split it asunder. Out of this general crisis comes a new social order; capitalist social relations are born.

Most of the countries of the world today are undergoing a feudal epoch. Practically all countries, other than those in Western Europe, the United States, Japan, Canada, New Zealand, or Australia can be characterized by a preponderance of landless peasants within the human population. Most of these nations are undergoing a transition, as witness the development of a wage earning class. This latter, however, is generally a small part of the working classes and is pretty much confined to government employment or to jobs in industries controlled by foreign capitalist corporations. The fact that these foreign companies and their governments exploit the people and their non-human materials

Special types of political economies

does not detract from the essentially feudal epoch in which these countries are now operating.

The capitalist society is indeed an international predator whose prey is all the different peoples undergoing social reproduction in all the historical epochs, at any given moment in real time throughout the entire non-capitalist world. To be sure, a particular capitalist nation may itself be prey of other capitalist nations.

The capitalist epoch has inflicted some of the most brutal invasions of human dignity.

The capitalist system

Capitalism is a type of social organization in which wealth has the form of a special type of commodity called "capital."

The people in this society are fractionated into two main classes. Members of the capitalist class are distinguished by their private ownership of capital. Members of the class of wage laborers are distinguished by their private ownership of one type of commodity only – a special type called "human energy."

A "commodity" is quite important in capitalist society. It is indeed a microcosm of the capitalist epoch. Its structure mirrors and reflects the joint operations of the five institutional mechanisms of capitalist social reproduction. We therefore need to define it and to elaborate on its essential attributes.

First and foremost, a commodity is a synthesis of two distinct material elements – laborers and food.

Second, each of the two commodity elements is created by human labor.

Third, the fusion of the two elements to form the synthesis is a result of the catalytic action of a special commodity called "money."

Fourth, the fission of the commodity into its two independent constituent elements is a result of the accumulation of the commodity elements and money as private property.

These four attributes of a commodity are sufficient to generate a wide variety of rather interesting results.

As synthesis of earth material elements, a commodity, too, has an earth material substratum. As such, its specific material form is determined by the relative magnitudes of its two material elements.

Special types of political economies

Thus, an infinite number of different commodities is capable of existence. Each specific commodity is uniquely associated with a specific material composition of the elements.

On the other hand, the quantitative magnitude of a commodity is determined by the absolute quantity of each of its material elements. Thus an infinite number of different quantities of the same commodity can be uniquely associated with the infinite number of possible common proportional changes in the two elements.

Laborers are created by human labor in the Internal Labor Process. The quantity of Internal Labor required to produce any given quantity of laborers is therefore an important attribute of the given quantity of commodity. We shall refer to this quantity of Internal Labor as "Input of Internal Labor." The Input of Internal Labor congealed in one unit quantity of laborers will be called the "Specific Labor" of laborers.

Food is created by human labor in the External Labor Process. The quantity of External Labor required to create food is therefore an important attribute of a commodity. We shall refer to this quantity of External Labor as "Input of External Labor." The Input of External Labor congealed in a unit quantity of food shall be called the "Specific Value of Food."

As synthesis of the two elements, a commodity represents an equilibrium of opposite-directed forces. The quantity of laborers within the synthesis is in motion, being distributed from the Internal Labor Process to the External Labor Process. Simultaneously, the quantity of food within the synthesis is in motion, being distributed from the External Labor Process to the Internal Labor Process. The forces acting on each, and thereby responsible for their motion, are Input of Internal Labor and Input of External Labor, respectively. The equilibrium is achieved by each of the elements being converted into money, the medium in which the distribution takes place. The catalytic action of the money medium brings about an equality between the two opposite-directed forces of human labor. This process involves (a) a conversion of the laborers into money, (b) a conversion of the food into money, and with (c) no apparent change in the form of the money medium. Of course, no apparent change in the form of the money medium must be dynamically interpreted as a conversion of money into money, because the money plays a very active role in the process.

Special types of political economies

The formation of the synthesis takes place in the two distributional processes. These types of commodity distribution shall be referred to as "Market" institutions, the peculiar form of distribution characteristic of capitalist society. In the markets, three important attributes of the commodity are the quantity of Internal Labor carried by the laborers, the quantity of External Labor carried by the food, and the common quantity of money into which the two elements are converted.

The quantity of Internal Labor in the market shall be referred to as the "Output of Internal Labor." This quantity is calculated by multiplying the Specific Labor of laborers times the quantity of laborers distributed in the market.

The quantity of External Labor in the market shall be referred to as "Output of External Labor." Its quantity is calculated by multiplying the specific value of food times the quantity of food distributed in the market.

The common money magnitude of the Output of Internal Labor or the Output of External Labor is referred to as "Exchange Value of Laborers" or "Exchange Value of Food," respectively. A unit of Exchange Value is called "Price" of the respective commodity.

At the conclusion of each market relation, each of the commodity elements is acquired as private property. Food is acquired as private property of laborers, to be used up in the Internal Labor Process. Laborers are acquired as private property of capitalists, to be used up in the External Labor Process. Money is accumulated as private property of capitalists to form part of their stock of personal material wealth.

It is now clear that a commodity is a rather complex and dynamic entity. Its definition spans the five institutional mechanisms of social reproduction in capitalist society. It is a material synthesis of laborers and food; it has a specific material form that is unlike either of its elements; it is Output of Internal Labor; it is Output of External Labor; it has a common money magnitude of its two labor outputs; it has an Input of Internal Labor which puts one of its elements into motion; it has an Input of External Labor which puts one of its elements into motion; finally, it carries a split personality. It is accumulated as private money wealth; but it must be returned to the market in its social role to restart the cycle of distribution, and hence lay the basis for the renewed cycle of Internal and External Labor, as well as accumulation of capital.

Special types of political economies

All these attributes which inhere in the commodity typify the continuing and dynamic tensions between members of the class of capitalists and members of the class of wage laborers. These tensions are indicative of the stability of the capitalist epoch of social reproduction; but they also manifest in bold outlines the volatile and potentially explosive possibilities inherent in the system.

The scenario goes something like this. The population of wage laborers exert Internal Labor upon themselves by using up their existing stocks of food. The result of this activity is the creation of the population of laborers. The labor so generated exerts a pressure upon the pre-existing population of laborers to send them in motion towards the External Labor Process. In an intermediary position between the two labor processes, in the market for human energy, the laborers encounter a money barrier, an inertial mass to be overcome before External Labor can be performed. The money absorbs their motion, thus bringing them to rest in the External Labor Process.

The laborers are put to work exerting External Labor to create food. The labor so generated exerts a pressure upon the pre-existing stocks of food to send them into motion towards the Internal Labor Process. In an intermediary position between the two labor processes, in the market for consumer goods, the food encounters a money barrier, the inertial mass that must be overcome before it can be used to generate Internal Labor. The money absorbs the motion of the food, thus bringing it to rest in the Internal Labor Process.

The energies of the laborers in the External Labor Process are used by their capitalist owners to generate labor for creating a new stock of food. Simultaneously, the food in the Internal Labor Process is consumed by laborers to generate labor for the creation of a new supply of laborers. The new laborers are accumulated as private property of laborers; the new food is accumulated as private property of capitalists; and the money, now sated with the results of its market role, is likewise accumulated as private property of capitalists.

All the conditions are now ripe for a potential repetition of the cycle of reproduction in the specifically capitalist mode.

From this rather detailed discussion of the nature of a commodity it becomes quite obvious that the money commodity plays a unique

Special types of political economies

role in the system. As a matter of fact, it is almost impossible to define a commodity without first assuming the existence of the money commodity. To avoid this obvious tautology, we can still define money in terms of its two constituent elements. It is the one commodity whose specific material form is dominated by neither of its two elements. Thus, as commodity, it has the form of neither of its elements.

As money commodity, when functioning within the markets, it has the properties of each of its elements; its social dimensions are in action. When functioning within the Process of Accumulation, however, it has the properties of neither of its elements; it is the "negation of the negation." In this function it brings the system of capitalist social reproduction to a halt.

Nevertheless, it is precisely the accumulation of wealth in the ultimate form of money capital that provides the individual motivation of capitalists, and thus the subjective motor which drives the system.

Among the roles of money is its function to provide a common metric for quantities of an infinite number of different material commodity forms. It can physically perform this role because, in common with all other commodities, it is a product of the same activity – human labor. Moreover, one of its specific functions is to serve as the medium in which commodities are distributed; that is to say, all commodities must have a legitimate money "stamp" as a necessary condition before they can be used by laborers or capitalists. The markets are the institutions where money performs this role. An important question, however, still remains as to how money actually measures the quantities of other commodities. Recall that the physical quantity of any commodity varies directly with the quantity of any one of its elements. In the language of the mathematician, the first partial derivative of the commodity's quantity, with respect to any one of its elements, is positive. Customarily one uses such things as number, crate, bushel, can, liter, gram, etc. to measure commodity quantity. Since every commodity has an earth material substratum, its quantity can be reduced to "weight." But we are still stuck with the commensurability of the different specific material forms of commodities. Five pounds of cotton may not be equivalent in the market sense to five pounds of gold.

Consider any two commodities, "A" and "B." We can determine

that the quantity of "A" is greater than the quantity of "B," if "A" has no less of one of its elements than "B," but has more of the second element than "B." Using "B" as a standard quantity, the subset of commodities, each of which has larger quantity than "B," satisfies the properties of "A" with respect to "B." Similarly, the subset "C" of commodities, each of which has smaller quantity than "B," stands in relation to "B" as "B" is to "A."

It follows that there exists a group, "D," of commodities, each of which has less of one element than "B," but more of the second element than "B." Among this group is a subset, "E," each of which has equal quantity as "B." Call this subset the "B"-isoquantity commodities.

For each constant multiple, "q," of the elements of "B," we can identify the "qB"-isoquantity subset of commodities. Each commodity in this latter subset has "q" times its "B"-isoquantity.

The quantity of any commodity, therefore, varies directly and in the same proportion as its "B"-isoquantity. At the same time the "B"-isoquantity identifies a subset of all the distinct types of commodities.

Now let "B" represent the money commodity. Quantities of all the different commodities can now be measured by their "money-isoquantity." All the special forms can now be converted into the equivalent quantities of each other, based on the relative quantities of their special materials which have the same money quantity.

The common activity out of which all commodities are created is human labor. But human labor, whether of the external or internal phase, is an activity performed by laborers. Labor, therefore, implies an interval of time within which the activity takes place. Time duration, then, is an important consideration in any labor metric.

As activity, however, human labor may be performed with different degrees of intensity. This factor likewise is an important consideration in any labor metric.

These two attributes of labor – time duration and intensity – come together in the physical quantity of the commodity and the specific material substance of the commodity, respectively. In other words, for a given intensity of labor, the quantity of a particular type of commodity varies directly with the duration of labor; for a given duration of labor, different types of commodities are generated by different intensities of labor.

Special types of political economies

Once the time period during which labor takes place is ended, the laboring activity expires; as activity performed by human laborers, it has disappeared. However, it creates a material commodity in whose physical quantity is congealed the duration of labor. On the other hand, the intensity of the labor which was performed manifests its concrete nature in the specific material substratum of the commodity.

It follows that the ratio of any two quantities of the same type of commodity is equal to the ratio of the quantities of labor congealed in them. Likewise, the ratio of the quantities of two different, but money-isoquantity, commodities reflects the inverse of the ratio of intensities of labor congealed in their materials.

If we now fix a certain quantity of money as the "Standard Unit of Measure" of commodity quantity or of the labor congealed in a commodity, the number of units of the standard contained in any quantity of money is unambiguous. For example, if the standard is one ounce of gold, then one pound of gold contains sixteen standard units.

The standard may be fixed by accident, custom, fiat, or law. In capitalist society it is fixed by the Political State, which monitors it continuously and vigorously regulates its use for insuring the inviolability of market relations as the legitimate method of acquisition of private proprietorship in someone else's commodity.

The quantity of labor congealed in a standard quantity of the money commodity is equal to a standard quantity of human labor. On the other hand, since money is the general form into which all specific commodities convert, the standard quantity of money also congeals the general intensity of human labor.

What all this means in terms of a labor metric is that money is not only a natural measure of the quantity of all the different commodities; it is also a measure of the quantity of human labor activity – the subjective element – of all commodities.

For example, if the standard unit of money is one ounce of gold and four hundred loaves of bread congeal the same quantity of labor as an ounce of gold; then one loaf of bread has a quantity of one-fourhundredth an ounce of gold; and the quantity of labor contained in the four hundred loaves of bread is equal to the quantity of labor contained in one standard unit of gold.

The importance of the money commodity is so pervasive in capitalist society that its roles need to be elaborated on. In one of these roles it gives the peculiar stamp to the processes of distribution in capitalist society. These processes are two markets – for human energy and for consumer goods.

A market is an institutional relationship between wage laborers on one pole and capitalists on the other pole. A member of each class comes to the market relation with a stock of privately owned commodities. Members of one class must be owners of money; these are called "buyers." Members of the other class must be owners of non-money commodities; these are called "sellers."

The sellers wish to acquire private property rights in the buyers' money. Simultaneously, the buyers wish to acquire private property rights in the sellers' non-money commodity. If the relationship is consummated, then a certain sum of money is ceded by the buyers to their opposite class – the sellers. At the same time, a certain quantity of non-money commodities is ceded by the sellers to the buyers.

The crucial act of the market relationship is that a money owner converts his private ownership of money into his private ownership of a non-money commodity. Simultaneously, the non-money commodity owner converts his private ownership of that commodity into his private ownership of money. Beneath the surface of these acts is the brute fact of a metamorphosis of the non-money commodity into money – a change of form of a special type of commodity into its general commodity form.

On a social level, the market relationship simulates the dialectics of private property. Private property rights of each party to the relation have been abrogated; simultaneously, private property rights of each have been reinstated. So long as the commodities exchanged are "equal" in some fundamental sense, then private property and its negation reside together in the body of the money form of the commodity. "Equality" of commodities in the markets is equality in terms of money-isoquantities.

Two types of markets can be identified, based on the possible role of buyer or seller, by a laborer or a capitalist. Laborers as sellers and capitalists as buyers distinguish the Market for Human Energy. Laborers as buyers and capitalists as sellers typify the Consumer Goods Market.

The distribution of human energy from the Internal Labor Process to the External Labor Process is accomplished in the mechanisms of the Market for Human Energy. In this market a laborer appears

Special types of political economies

as a private owner of a stock of human energy. He confronts a capitalist who comes as private owner of a stock of money. The capitalist acquires private ownership of some portion of that human energy by ceding his private property rights in a certain sum of money. Simultaneously, the laborer cedes his private property rights in some portion of his human energy and acquires private property in a sum of money. The bundle of human energy acquired by the capitalist is identically what the laborer gave up. Similarly, the stock of money ceded by the capitalist is identically what the laborer acquired. A purchase and a sale of human energy have been simultaneously consummated.

Money in this relation is a special form of exchange value. It is "wage income" to the laborer and "wage cost" to the capitalist. The "wage rate" is the price or specific exchange value of the money; that is to say, it is the wage cost divided by the quantity of human energy purchased. The human energy given up by the laborer is the specific labor multiplied by the quantity of human energy exchanged.

There is no rule that establishes an identical wage rate to be offered by different capitalists to the same laborer, nor by the same capitalist to different laborers. At the same time, there is no rule that establishes an identical Specific Labor among the different laborers. Each capitalist comes to market with a free will, with his privately owned External Labor Process to operate, and with other individual characteristics that distinguish him from all the other capitalists. Each worker comes to market with a free will, with a specific number of family members to be reproduced, and with other characteristics that distinguish her/him from all other wage laborers. Hence, the specific labor in any given transaction may be greater than, equal to, or less than the wage rate; specific labor is subject to a non-singular distribution among all wage laborers; wage rate is subject to a non-singular distribution within a unit of External Labor; and average wage rate offered by a capitalist is subject to a non-singular distribution among all capitalists.

This recitation raises the possibility of apparent chaos, manifested in the wide variations in the terms of settlement within the Market for Human Energy. It is indeed precisely that. There is a relative free-for-all in which power and guile and luck and chance and greed and dog-eat-dog selfishness and a host of other human frailties come to bear in these interactions between laborers and

Special types of political economies

capitalists. Other influences come from associations of capitalists, associations of workers, incursions of the Political State. Yet, on the level of the national political economy there still may be a predictable systematic outcome.

The distribution of consumer goods from the External Labor Process to the Internal Labor Process is accomplished through the mechanism of the Market for Consumer Goods. In this market a capitalist appears as a private owner of a stock of consumer goods. He confronts a laborer who comes as private owner of a stock of money. The laborer acquires private ownership of some portion of those consumer goods by ceding his private property rights in a certain sum of money. Simultaneously, the capitalist cedes his private property rights in some portion of his consumer goods and acquires private property rights in a sum of money. The stock of consumer goods acquired by the laborer is identically what the capitalist gave up. Similarly, the stock of money ceded by the laborer is identically what the capitalist acquired. A purchase and a sale of consumer goods have been simultaneously consummated.

Money in this relationship is a special form of exchange value generally called "consumer expenditures" to the laborer and "consumer sales revenues" to the capitalist. The price or specific exchange value of the consumer goods is the consumer expenditures divided by the quantity of consumer goods purchased. The value of the consumer goods is the specific value multiplied by the quantity sold.

There is no rule that establishes an identical price of consumer goods offered by different laborers to the same capitalist, nor by the same laborer to different capitalists. At the same time, there is no rule that establishes an identical specific value among the different capitalists. Each laborer comes to market with a free will, with a specific Internal Labor Process to operate, and with other familial characteristics that distinguish her/him from all other laborers. Each capitalist comes to market with a free will, with a specific stock of capital to be reproduced, and with other characteristics that distinguish him from all other capitalists. Therefore, Specific Value in any given transaction may be greater than, equal to, or less than the price; Specific Value is subject to a non-singular distribution among all capitalists; Price is subject to a non-singular distribution among all laborers purchasing from the same capita-

Special types of political economies

list; and average price paid by laborers to a given capitalist is subject to a non-singular distribution among all capitalists.

These facts raise the possibility of a staggering variety of terms of settlement within the Market for Consumer Goods. It is precisely a free-for-all jungle in which private gain, luck, chance, chicanery, power, influence, and all manner of devious motivations prevail between laborers and capitalists. Other influences such as consumer's advocacy groups, collusion among capitalists, regulations of the Political State also come into play. Yet, on the national level there still may be a predictable and systematic outcome to all this.

Once the laborers and capitalists have completed one of the market operations, the non-money commodity is taken into the appropriate Labor Process to be used to create its opposite, but complementary, commodity. In particular, at the conclusion of the activities in the Market for Human Energy the capitalist is in an effective position to use his now privately owned human energy to generate External Labor, which in turn creates capital.

Recall that human energy is carried within the person of the laborer. Its purchase, therefore, implies that the laborer must physically accompany it into the capitalist's bailiwick. The actual way in which the capitalist alienates his private property in the human energy from the person of the laborer is to put the laborer to work, exerting that energy against some pre-existing stock of capital, external to the person of the laborer, to produce capital in accordance with a preconceived plan designed by the capitalist. In other words, the laborer's act of performing External Labor is precisely the method by which the capitalist uses the human energy which is now the capitalist's private property, legally acquired previously in the Market for Human Energy.

The relation between capitalist and laborer in the External Labor Process is one of capitalist dominance over a subordinate laborer. Under these circumstances the laborer must be managed. This means that the capitalist must subordinate the will of the laborer to the capitalist's aims, directing it to perform the tasks required for the production of capital. The method of production, the specific task within the detailed division of labor to be performed by the laborer, and the degree of intensity of External Labor to be extracted from the laborer are all legally within the prerogatives of the capitalist and are determined by the conscious exercise of

Special types of political economies

the capitalist's will. Furthermore, and absolutely important, is the fact that the product of the laborer's External Labor is the private property of the capitalist and not of the laborer. Here is historic irony; the material product of the laborer's efforts belongs to someone else.

Internal Labor depends partly on a certain quantity of consumer goods in the possession of the laborer and his family. The acquisition of these goods by the laborer is accomplished by purchase in the Market for Consumer Goods. Once so legally acquired the laborer uses the goods in the Internal Labor Process by having his family consume them upon their persons, in accordance with a preconceived plan whose result is the creation of human energy. The act of Internal Labor is determined by the conscious application of the laborer's will. It is the laborer and her/his family members who determine the degree of intensity of Internal Labor which will be exerted.

The human energy produced as a result of Internal Labor is congealed in the persons of the members of the laborer's family. It is their private property and is an integral part of their bodies and souls. The newly created human energy now resides in the pre-existing family members; but part of it may also reside in newly created family members – new-born human babies.

The Process of Accumulation of Wealth must be such as to reproduce the capitalist epoch. This is partly successful so long as the only commodity laborers accumulate as their own private property is nothing other than human energy. This condition can be met if the sum total of wages paid to all laborers by all capitalists in the market for human energy is exactly equal to the sum total of all consumer expenditures made by all laborers to all capitalists in the consumer goods market. This is the "Law of the Markets" or, more precisely, the "Special Law of Conservation of Labor Output."

Reproduction of the capitalist epoch also requires that capitalists must accumulate capital as their own private property. This can take place if each capitalist can acquire from other capitalists, by bartering away part of his own product, in such a way that (a) the original quantities of all the specific capitals necessary for operating his External Labor Process are not diminished, (b) any change in his own product inventory is exactly in accordance with his preconceived plan, and (c) his stock of money capital has increased over the original stock.

A necessary condition for these results to take place is that the Law of the Markets holds; and that the total quantity of External Labor generated by all laborers exactly equals the total quantity of Internal Labor generated by all members of wage laboring families. This is the "Law of Production," or, more precisely, the "General Law of Conservation of Labor Input."

The two laws imply an equality between the quantity of labor accumulated by laborers in the Internal Labor Process and the quantity of labor accumulated by capitalists in the External Labor Process. This is the "Law of Accumulation of Capital," or, more precisely, the "Special Law of Conservation of Labor Inertia."

Finally, the dominant form of capital – money – must be accumulated out of the synthesis of some of the newly created human energy and some of the newly created non-money capital. This is the condition which restarts the cycle of market distribution of commodities, which in turn makes possible the next phase in the generation of Internal and External Labor, both as commodity using and commodity producing activities.

The principal function of the Political State is to exert the national forces which preserve private proprietorship in the ownership of commodities. It must therefore enforce the rules of market distribution. It must preserve the rights of private ownership of human energy by capitalists within the External Labor Process. It must preserve the rights of private proprietorship of laborers in ownership of consumer goods within the Internal Labor Process. Finally, it must enforce the rights of capitalists to privately accumulate wealth in the form of capital.

The Political State is primarily a servant of the class of capitalists. The distribution of private ownership of capital among the various capitalists mirrors and reflects the distribution of state power among them. Mammoth capital stocks owned by some individual capitalists reflect the extent of state power wielded by such capitalists. Large corporations are prime examples. Agglomerations of capitalists, based on commonly perceived interests, are not to be ruled out. Eastern banking interests and south-western oil interests in the United States, and trade associations are examples of this.

On the basis of these considerations one may observe in the real world a capitalist political state pursuing the private interests of some subsets of the capitalist class rather than the class as a whole. It may also appear at times to be torn among conflicting interests of different blocs of capitalists, acting as some kind of mediator. Still at other times it may be observed to be acting contrary to the interests of all capitalists – if only temporarily. This variety of observations has led to a great confusion about the nature of the state in capitalist society. Nevertheless, whatever it is observed to be doing at any given moment, such doing is but a specific tactical method of carrying out its primary function of preserving capitalist wealth and the capitalist relations which that wealth generates.

Among its functions, the Political State must enforce the rules of the Internal Labor Process. Wage workers' private ownership of the newly created human energy must be inviolate. This fact has led to some notions about the liberal nature of the state. Private ownership of human energy implies private ownership of one's person. Slavery or feudal exploitation have to be ruled out by exercise of state power. Protection of the civil rights of the laborers is the tactic for carrying out this function. In reality, however, this state function generally turns on enforcing rules of behavior governing interrelations among members of the class of wage laborers themselves. The halls of justice are overwhelmed with trials and punishments of laborers for crimes against one another. Murder, arson, thievery, rape, assault are endemic to the working class against its own members. The vast army of domestic police forces, backed up by the National Guard (in the United States) and other armed forces, stand at the ready to keep the will of these people from exploding in ways inimical to capitalist private property relations.

The Political State is obligated in a most important way to preserve capitalist private ownership and control of human energy within the External Labor Process. Thus, it is an unabashed partisan of the capitalists in their domineering role over laborers. The act of alienating this human energy from laborers by working them is quite unnatural. Workers must necessarily rebel against the subordination of their will to that of an alien. This rebellion must be neutralized, kept within controllable limits so that the capitalists may use what is legitimately their own private property. Never mind that it resides within the bodies and souls of the wage laborers. The intensity with which their External Labor is extracted

Special types of political economies

is a measure of the forces of the state power which keeps them under control.

The Political State must rigidly enforce the rules of market distribution at all costs. It is precisely the market relations which make possible the capitalist mode of labor. One market legitimately sets the terms on which laborers are employed – how many will be employed, and at what wage incomes. The other market determines the terms by which the laborers will survive – how much consumer goods they may purchase with their wage incomes for their personal survival.

As a unity, then, the two markets set the preconditions for Internal and External Labor. Thus, they are crucial mechanisms that determine the rate at which laborers are exploited. And since it is enforced by the Political State, the rate of exploitation is legitimized. Stealing is virtuous, provided it is done in accordance with the rules of the capitalist market game.

The unity of the markets, after all, determines the percentage of the commodity produced by the laborer which she/he will receive. Under the slave regime the slave receives nothing. Whatever food she/he is given still belongs to the slave master because the slave is the private property of the slave master. In the feudal epoch the landless peasant receives a stipulated percentage of the fruits of his labor, generally set by prearrangement at less than 50 but greater than zero per cent. In the capitalist epoch, however, this percentage sharing gets blurred. The wage rate differs among individuals within a given capitalist's External Labor Process; average wage rate paid by a capitalist varies among the various capitalists; price paid by workers for their consumer goods varies among workers, depending upon the capitalists with whom they are relating in the relevant market.

In any case, the total quantity of consumer goods which all wage workers can purchase with their combined wage incomes is a given percentage of the total quantity of capital produced by these workers for all capitalists in the External Labor Process. This percentage remains rather stable over long periods of time and is generally less than 100 per cent, but greater than 50 per cent.

In the case of an individual laboring family, the lesser is its percentage share relative to the national average, the greater is its rate of exploitation in the generation of External Labor. Simultaneously, therefore, such a family must exert greater than average intensity of Internal Labor to make the pittance of consumer goods reproduce its family members.

The imposition of the powers of the Political State in the maintenance of market relations is tantamount to legitimizing the rate of exploitation of the class of wage laborers by the class of capitalists.

Finally, the Political State must preserve the right of capitalists to privately accumulate capital wealth. The right of capitalists to transform wage laborers and their material means of survival into capitalist private property must be enforced at all costs if the cycle of reproduction is to be restarted.

The inherent contradictions of the capitalist epoch are many and varied. Private property rights in the ownership of commodities separate the wage workers from their material means of survival. The synthesizing forces which bring the two into contact are the markets. Individual workers, therefore, have no guarantee that they will be successful market operators; automatic employment is out of the question. Thus, any unsuccessful attempt at employment precludes such a worker from legitimate claims on her/his material means of survival. Of great importance also is the possibility that even if successful in getting employment, there is no guarantee that the wage income will be adequate legally to claim a bundle of consumer goods that can provide the normal needs of reproduction of the worker's family members. No wage incomes and relatively low wage incomes are real possibilities that characterize capitalist society. Unemployment, low incomes, and the attendant material poverty and deprivation leave a significant number of the laboring population in a rather precarious position. In effect, they are legal outcasts from the realms of capitalist relations, with one foot mired in the grave.

The heart of the capitalist contradictions, however, is to be located in the very nature of capital itself. It contains two opposing forces, equal in extent, and growing in magnitude over time. The unity of the two markets signifies the synthesizing forces, the social pressures of private property, which rivet the class of workers to their material means of survival, under the iron fist of the Political State.

On the other hand, the extent of these synthesizing forces is matched by the extent of the analytic forces of human labor in the people's struggle to shatter the bonds of exploitation. Matching the market forces are the analytic forces of Internal Labor, pushing

Special types of political economies

relentlessly in the direction of reproducing the people and their energies. Likewise, matching the market forces are the analytic forces of External Labor, pushing in the opposite direction of wresting out of mother earth the people's material means of survival.

In the meantime, the accumulation of capital wealth continues in increasing magnitude over time. This enables the capitalists to restart the cycle of labor by reimposing market relations upon the backs of the growing population of laborers, with greater intensity and relatively less employed workers. The alternating heartbeats of Internal and External Labor of the people must therefore proceed at progressively greater intensities. The mass of unemployed and dead laborers grows apace with the mass of accumulating capital. Poverty among the people matches the increasing capital wealth among the capitalists.

This continuing and necessary contradiction is at the bottom of the capitalist crisis. The crisis appears regularly with the periodicity of labor. Over the long term, in step with the changing forms of capital as it is quantitatively accumulated, the balance of forces is intermittently thrown out of kilter. The extent of accumulation of capital ultimately calls forth an intensity of labor that is beyond the forces of the markets to contain. Prometheus shatters the chains of Vulcan which riveted him to the rock of capitalism.

Symptoms of the general crisis are the tremendous accumulations of capital, matched with a tremendous accumulation of unemployed laboring families within the population. At some level of critical mass, the dead weight of these laborers overwhelms the system and crushes it underfoot. The die is cast. The capitalist epoch comes to an end.

The socialist system

The Marxian hypothesis projected a socialist epoch as the successor to capitalism in the progress of human evolution. In the real world thus far the facts are not yet sufficiently clear to verify this speculation.

After the revolution of 1917 the leadership of the Soviet Union proclaimed a socialist regime. Following on World War II, some of the countries of Eastern Europe launched a so-called people's

Special types of political economies

democracy drive as a deliberate transitional form of society which would by-pass capitalism on the way to socialism. In later years the People's Republic of China was born out of the defeat of the Kuo Min Tang. Under Mao a vigorous revolution was put in place in an attempt to forge a socialist state, within a reasonable period of time, out of the feudal conditions of that vast population of Chinese people. On the African continent various people's democracies have been proclaimed in such places as Angola, Mozambique, and Tanzania. In the Americas, Cuba has proclaimed such a regime; Nicaragua may not be far behind.

It is up to the astute student to study these cases carefully in order better to understand how they fit into the drama of social development.

A digression on race

The object of our endeavors is ultimately to form a clear understanding of the historical forces which have transformed the black American population. We cannot even begin to approach this task without commenting on the concept of "race."

This concept has been used in the literature for a number of centuries. Particularly during the period of the Atlantic slaving operations, Europeans and their offshoots in the Americas have proclaimed distinctions among peoples based on different racial stocks. Africans were different from Europeans.

If it stopped there, no more need be said. But wherever the racial distinction is proclaimed it is very curious that it is always done effectively by popular writers and scholars of a group of people who dominate over another group. The subordinate group is not only a different racial stock, but it is an "inferior" racial stock; superiority-inferiority syndrome is endemic to the concept.

It is also quite curious that the popular writers and scholars who proclaim racial hierarchies are generally in the pay of a yet smaller group among the superior race who dominate the political economy through their ownership and control of the most important materials of wealth. Thus, the inferiority of one race is demonstrated conclusively at two levels of proof.

The ruling class within the dominant group exploits the inferior racial group at such levels of intensity as to leave them with only the barest material means of survival. A significant portion of the fruits of their labor is expropriated by the ruling class. Thus, their materially deprived condition emanating from the inhuman theft of their labor, is positive empirical proof of their "inferiority."

On a second level, the working-class members of the dominant group are exploited by the ruling class at rates significantly below those of the inferior race. These working-class members of the dominant group are moreover employed as the civil servant "policemen" who directly apply the physical force of the Political State to whip the inferior race into line to accept the legalities of their own exploitation. In some cases they wear official uniforms; in other cases they wear white bed sheets; in still other cases they join together as riot mobs. In all cases, however, they are the instruments of ruling-class brutality against the will of the inferior race. In this role the working-class members of the dominant group are empirically observed to be materially better off, and, therefore, superior to the inferior race. Never mind their status with respect to the ruling class. Such status is blurred in the literature under the guise that it is only a matter of time or individual initiative before some working-class members of the dominant group will move into the ranks of the ruling class. The route to that end may come from marriage, exceptional scholarship, great military prowess, undetected criminal activity, and the like. In general, it comes from a small group of those who commit themselves to be the unbending, true and loyal servants of the ruling class, serving them in positions of trust and responsibility – overseeing the counting and the preservation of their wealth.

The serious student who seeks truth and clarity cannot debauch her/his studies by using the concept of race. It is too contaminated with the filth of deceitful scholarship. It is analytically empty, devoid of the elementary canons of scientific methodology. When applied to black people its vicious consequences are quite obvious.

If race is an empty concept, then what is a black person? Surely, if we try to identify blacks by race we have to resort immediately to their skin color as a possible criterion. No success can be achieved here. Black people spawn all the colors of the rainbow and much more besides. Their blood has been tainted with the venom of the vermin slave masters who forcibly injected their polluted seeds into slave women's wombs. The rape of black womanhood now appears visible in the panorama of colors among

Special types of political economies

black people. But the power of blackness is such that just one droplet of black blood still marks the offspring as black.

The only way to identify black people in the United States is to use criteria which unambiguously distinguish them from other people. No one criterion will do. Indeed, we think that a combination of a certain five criteria are necessary, even if not sufficient. These are (1) common origins on the continent of Africa; (2) common history of exploitation as a homogeneous slave working class in North America for more than two hundred and fifty years; (3) common exploitation as a more or less homogeneous class of landless peasants for approximately one hundred years in the southern United States; (4) common experience of exploitation as a homogenous wage laboring class since the last decade or so of their history; and (5) conscious individual acceptance of being black.

Using these criteria it becomes obvious that we are looking at a people who have been bound together in a socially reproducing embrace throughout the centuries. They have been linked in a stable and continuing bond of producing and consuming their material means of survival; simultaneously they have been linked in a family mode of dying and borning and socializing their young to perpetuate themselves as a people. And all of this has been done with each other, to the general exclusion of all others.

On the other hand, they have been exploited by aliens throughout their history in America. They have been a working class in three distinct historical epochs. They have been slaves, landless peasants, and wage laborers. In each epoch they have maintained their identity as a people apart.

In the rest of the book we shall try to analyze black people in these terms – how they originated, how they have survived as a people apart, and how they have been transformed from one epoch to another in their continuing saga.

3 Special cases of black American political economies

The overriding factor which generates any special case of black American political economy is the distinctiveness of the black people themselves. While they have been "Americans" for centuries, nevertheless, they have generally borne offspring through unions between black men and black women. They have had the primary burden of rearing their babies to full maturity, steeping them in their own folkways and mores, communicating with them in their own peculiar language, instilling in them their own concepts of morality, and generally socializing them into the human condition in accordance with their own designs.

To be sure, the persistence of their distinctiveness was aided and abetted by alien marauders. Over the last four and a half centuries relatively small bands of Europeans or their offshoots in the Americas have entrapped them into systems of social reproduction that congeal the greater part of their External Labors into massive accumulations of material wealth for the alien invaders. As a consequence, they have had to match those doses of External Labors with equal doses of Internal Labors, fueled by extremely small quantities of the material means of their survival. This has translated, throughout their existence to date, into tremendous numbers of black babies issuing from their loins but succumbing to the ravages of death in record numbers. Low survival rate of the black population has been the historical reality.

In short, blacks have been in the last four and a half centuries an almost homogeneous working class, exploited by non-black ruling classes of relatively small membership, who have owned and controlled their material means of survival. Meantime, members of these ruling classes have consciously erected impassable kinship barriers between them and their black victims in order to better exploit them. Hence, the time is yet to come when black people will reproduce with other people as an indistinguishable population.

Blacks have also reproduced within common geographic domains. They were forcibly joined together in the geographic domain of the slave dungeons of Africa prior to shipment to the Americas. These hell-holes were essentially their first geographic domains under alien control. They subsequently shared the cramped quarters in the stinking holds of the slavers' ships in the passage across the Atlantic Ocean. These ships upon the ocean were their second geographic domain. They were put ashore astride the banks of the James River and then at all the major Atlantic ports of entry to the British North American tobacco colonies. Some of their kinsfolk landed at points all over Central and South America, as well as Canada, Mexico, and the Caribbean basin. This was their third geographic domain. Today they reside throughout the United States and its territories. Their geographic domain is now shared with all the non-black Americans.

In real time they have been a distinctive people sharing a common geographic domain for at least four and one half centuries. This rather long span of years has produced a sufficiently large number of generations of black men and women and children to shape their peculiar population traits.

Throughout the passage of real time, however, they have reproduced in at least three historical epochs. They have been subject to the slave masters' autocratic direction of their labor without any compensation therefor; they have husbanded the landlords' soils for a small share of the fruits of their own labor; they have toiled in the capitalists' firms for below average money wages. Furthermore, they have experienced these three historical epochs at different intervals in real time compared to other non-black Americans.

Since they have not spawned a ruling class in any of the historical epochs through which they have passed, they have been under the gun of an alien Political State. The unbearable pressures of the distribution processes, engendered by the Political State's application of overwhelming force, have provided the legal basis for their exploitation in each of the epochs. Their lot has therefore been, in each of the epochs, a continuing struggle to liberate themselves. They have obviously been successful in their struggles; however, it

Special cases of black American political economies

has been their sorry fate that another small band of aliens has been waiting in strategic locations at the conclusion of each epoch to ensnare them into a new form of labor exploitation.

Finally, the outside world of black people has been quite different from that of any other people. At the beginning of the epoch of slavery they were hunted and gathered and sold as commodities by profit making capitalist corporations. In the case of Great Britain, this was precisely the period of the transition from feudalism to capitalism. Slaving operations and slave exploitation in the colonies were at once the most important sources of primitive capital accumulation. These were the motors that turned the wheels of industry. They were indeed the chief capital producing sectors of the nascent British capitalist External Labor Process.

During the slave epoch in the colonies and later in the free United States, blacks labored under a system of exploitation quite different from their non-black laboring brothers and sisters. During the sharecropping era, blacks labored under a system of exploitation that was shared by some of their non-black brothers and sisters. However, the majority of non-black workers were either working for wages or were soon to be employed in the capitalist enterprises throughout the country. Blacks were not to experience this condition for a hundred years after freedom from slavery.

Today, for the first time, the blacks are an integral part of the class of wage laborers. The legacy of separate identity as a people, and their late coming to wage laborer status will require a transitional period before unity comes to all workers.

The focus on special cases of black political economies must be the specific ways in which black people have been reproduced as a black population in each of the various historical epochs through which they have passed. The central theme should be how the five institutional mechanisms of social reproduction (External Labor, Internal Labor, the two distribution processes, the Process of Accumulation of Wealth) have played themselves out in the black survival drama.

This type of formulation effectively places black people on center stage of world history and world political-economic development. Their experience spans the record of human existence from some three million years ago on the plains and river valleys of Mother Africa to the modern-day, twentieth-century capitalist North America. The dynamics of these developments intertwine with, and

Special cases of black American political economies

give substance and color to, the origins and growth of Western European capitalism and all the havoc which that system has since inflicted upon humankind.

Four leading issues frame the study of the special cases. Who are these people at this very moment in real time? How and where and in what type of world did they originate? What were the historical dynamics that transformed them over the course of the centuries? What is to become of them; what is their final destiny?

The 1980 Census of Population of the United States should report the existence of some 27.2 million black Americans, living in every region – north, south, east, west – of the country. Few live on farms. The overwhelming majority reside in small, densely populated ghetto enclaves near the central business districts of the cities in the larger metropolitan areas. They are the most urbanized group of a primarily urban population.

(For the most part they are members of the class of wage laborers.) Very few own businesses of any substantial size. (Most depend for employment – and therefore survival – on non-black owned business firms or non-black controlled government bureaucracies. A good number serve in the armed forces.)

They are generally considered to be one of the poorest segments of the population. They get the least prestigious jobs and at the lowest levels of money wages. The quantity and quality of the consumer goods which they can afford to purchase for their survival are very circumscribed.

Many of them are without employment; these depend for their existence on public grants of money or commodities such as aid to families with dependent children, food stamps, rent subsidies, medicare, medicaid. A good number subsist in prisons. A not insignificant number are permanent guests of hospitals, mental institutions, and old folks' homes. A few receive social security benefits, having been extremely lucky to have retired from "covered" employment. Others simply rely on the largesse of friends, relatives, and acquaintances.

They collectively give birth to more than half a million live babies annually. If one adds the number aborted, they gestate, to varying degrees of completion of term, close to one million black babies a year.

The black babies they bring into the world constitute more than fifteen per cent of the total for the nation. Yet, the surviving

Special cases of black American political economies

population of black people stand at slightly more than eleven per cent of the national total. Those potential members of the population who do not now form part of the survivors represent the excessive rate of decay, of death, of black people compared to their non-black counterparts. This is indeed a direct measure of the rate of exploitation of black people's labor; the ravages of black External Labor, coupled with the meager means of survival returned to them, take excessive tolls in lives of blacks of all ages.

More than a half of the new black babies given birth come into families without the presence of a husband. The burden of birthing, of tending to, of socializing, and of rearing to maturity bear inordinately heavily on the black mothers. Unemployment and low pay, if employed, are visited upon black women in such a way that they become the most economically downtrodden segment of people within the nation. Yet their responsibilities for borning and nurturing the black population for survival are the most onerous of tasks faced by any other group of people in the nation.

It was not proclaimed in heaven that black Americans shall be a class of wage laborers from the beginning of time and for evermore. No, indeed. Their present wage laborer status is the end result of a long and protracted series of historical processes which transformed them on the North American continent from slave, to sharecropper, to wage laborer.

They were involuntarily wrenched from the womb of the black Mother Africa and brought to the shores of the James River in Virginia in 1619. They continued to be brought in a trickle until the end of the seventeenth century. Then they began to flood the British tobacco colonies until 1865. Throughout the entire period they provided, without an ounce of compensation, the labor which was to form the basis of wealth in the colonizing metropole of Great Britain as well as to generate the "primitive" capital for the nascent American business classes of New England and the Middle Atlantic colonies.

The capitalist revolution in America, popularly called the Civil War, dealt the death blow to the class of slave owners and to the economic epoch of slavery over which it presided. At the same time it established the political hegemony of the capitalist class over the machinery of the national political state.

Although they gave their blood and their labor in the struggle to overthrow the slaveocracy, the reward of the freed blacks was rather cruel. (They were not brought into the new capitalist system as capitalists; nor were they brought in as wage laborers. Instead, they were captured by a new band of aliens and made victims of another system of exploitation. A system of black sharecropping was put into place and was to prevail for another hundred years in a special enclave called the "black belt" of the southern United States.) The system forced black External Labor to produce cotton – and to a lesser extent sugar, rice, tobacco, hemp, and indigo – for a relatively few non-black landowners and a parasitic class of merchants.

During the sharecropping period and under the most difficult conditions of labor exploitations, blacks struggled to liberate themselves by seeking possession of land through peaceful means. Fifty years later black land ownership reached a zenith of some fifteen million acres.

At the same time that land ownership had reached a peak, the nation witnessed the beginnings of a flood tide of black migrants, voluntarily leaving the land to seek employment in the cities of the nation. (This voluntary move was one of the most dramatic in the history of humankind and represented the visible moments of a black social revolution in the making – a revolution which was to transform the black sharecropper into a black wage laborer.)

The revolution was finally consummated at the end of the 1960s. The end of an epoch and the beginning of a new one was marked by a frontal assault against the legal superstructure of southern Jim Crow arrangements – segregated schools, segregated public facilities, racially restricted voting rights, racially motivated employment practices, segregated transportation conveyances. The assault was led by the Civil Rights Movement. In truth, this movement was the tail end of a revolutionary process which had been in progress for at least fifty years earlier. It not only marked the successful end of the sharecropping system of economic exploitation, with all its social and political baggages, but it also established the necessary legal basis for the existence of a class of black wage laborers. That is to say, it laid the foundations for embedding into the constitution, supporting statutes, and administrative practices the concept of equal protection of black workers under the law, the indisputable right of private proprietorship of the black laborer in her/his ability to work, the right to sell that ability on

Special cases of black American political economies

the open market to the highest bidder for a money wage and not for a direct share of the product of the black worker's labor.

By the beginning of the decade of the 1970s black Americans entered upon a new phase in their social reproduction. For the first time they had become a class of wage laborers, separated from their means of production – land – and from their elemental material means of consumption – food. Thus, they became dependent on wage employment by non-black corporations and government agencies for their survival.

Blacks have thus come in recent years to represent the last great reproducible segment of the general American wage working class. They are stamped with a special identity that came out of their unique historical experiences of economic oppression in America. These experiences involved a set of circumstances never before experienced by any other segment of the wage working class.

This last coming of blacks to the wage laborer class, coupled with their unique identity, will continue for some time to play a significant role in their future destiny.

Our projected study of the special cases of black American political economies will proceed along the lines suggested by the framework we have outlined above. It will first study the origins of blacks in the many and varied societies in Africa prior to the Atlantic slaving operations and the centuries preceding the formal colonization of Africa by the Europeans.

The succeeding phase of the study will concern itself with black slavery in the so-called "new world." The Atlantic slaving operations will be viewed as an essential External Labor sector of British capitalism which played a most fundamental role in the process of primitive capital accumulation. The exploitation of black slave labor in the British North American tobacco colonies will be analyzed for its role in fueling the rapid and sustained growth of British capitalism. Finally, the exploitation of black slave labor in the cotton growing states of the south will be analyzed for its critical contribution to the primitive capital accumulation in New England and the Middle Atlantic states.

The study continues with an analysis of the system of black sharecropping in the black belt counties of the south from the end of the Civil War to the end of the 1960s. The conditions under which the system was put into place, the mechanics of black sharecropping labor exploitation, the specific channels of expropriation of black labor for ultimate accumulation in the northern capitalist coffers, the great migration as social revolution against the system, and the ultimate destruction of sharecropping as an economic reality – all of these topics will come in for detailed analysis. The stage will then be set for a look at the present system under which black laborers now toil.

The direct exploitation of black wage laborers under the capitalist system will form an important area of study. Black unpaid labor as a significant basis for the extent of capital wealth formation will be the key issue.

Finally we must indulge some speculations about the future destiny of black Americans. In light of the understanding of the dynamics of history we shall try to project the course of their evolution in the centuries yet to come.

4 African origins of black Americans, 1450–1865

One of the major characteristics which distinguishes black Americans from all other Americans is their common origin on the continent of Africa. Their coming to the so-called new world was a function of European slaving operations, beginning about the middle of the fifteenth century and continuing unabated until sometime after the middle of the nineteenth century. During these four centuries those Africans who were destined to become black Americans were more directly the result of British slaving and British establishment of slave colonies in North America. This does not mean, however, that the British efforts in this sordid business can be separated from the same activities by Spain, Portugal, Netherlands, France, and other European countries. All these inhuman and piratical ventures were so interlocked that it is not possible to single out just one phase as the culprit.

The crucial issue in studying the origins in real time of black Americans is to identify the conditions within the first historical epoch that launched them as a population apart. We need to get a grasp of the forces which impinged on them as they were uprooted from the soil out of which they were fashioned. A related issue is the need to uncover the circumstances within their domestic political economies that made it possible for the Western Europeans to turn the African continent into a "warren for the commercial hunting of black skins."

Perhaps no other people and geographic area have received such a distorted treatment of their history as the African people and the African continent. We shall have to use some introspection, some logic, some smattering of documented facts, some empirical knowledge of other people similarly situated, and some theoretical

African origins of black Americans

applications in order to reconstruct a plausible picture of the structure of African societies prior to the Western European encroachment. This is not an easy task.

We must never lose sight of the fact that the process of slave hunting and slave shipments continued apace with the establishment and exploitation of black slave labor in the new world for more than four centuries. The point here is that one of the overriding motives for slaving was the establishment of a system of social reproduction of the slave in which fully one hundred per cent of her/his labor would be exploited for the benefit of people other than the slave. A related motive was, of course, the commercial profits to be made by the original slave hunters from the sale of the slaves.

It is clear that conditions within the various African societies during the four centuries of slaving operations laid the foundations for the defining characteristics of the blacks who came as slaves. Their African origins, therefore, cover not only these four centuries, but also the entire period from the origins – perhaps some three million or so years ago – of human people themselves.

It must be appreciated that Africa is an extremely large continent – not a country. By any standards of physical environment, biological entities, and social possibilities, Africa is quite an interesting and complex place. Its deserts, forests, mountains, rivers, and other physical features boggle the imagination in terms of their sheer size and overpowering presence. While mostly tropical, its climate varies through the whole range from excruciatingly hot to very frigid, depending upon the time of day and the physical properties of the location.

Probably more than a thousand languages are spoken. Although many of these may be traceable to a relatively small number of root tongues, nevertheless, the variations are indications of variations among the peoples and their historical pasts. Indeed, we must emphasize that when the Europeans came there were literally thousands of political aggregations of black people throughout the African continent, each with its own mode of social organization, its own unique historical background, its own language, its own complex of customs and institutions, its own territorial integrity.

From the evidence, it would appear that the types of wealth endemic to African societies at the middle of the fifteenth century were many and varied in form.

Among some people, common ownership of the fruits of the people's External Labor and common responsibility for the Internal Labor of rearing the children to maturity prevailed.

At the same time, among other people, the major form of wealth appeared to be human people themselves – slaves owned by a class of slave owners. In some of these cases the vast array of other material symptoms of wealth dazzled the imagination. Large standing armies, clad in glistening metals and leather and mounted on the finest horses, were visible indicators of the political power of the ruling classes. Stores of gold and salt and silks and other exotic materials were common in these societies among the slave owners. In short, the material power of the ruling classes in these societies marked the extent of accumulation of slave labor.

In other areas among other people there was privately owned wealth in the form of food. The immediate evidence for identifying these societies is the absence of slavery, but also the presence of powerful landowners who dominate the society by wielding unchallenged political power. In contrast, one would observe in these societies a relatively large class of landless peasants whose labor on the soil produced all the material goods.

Finally, there is sufficient evidence of what appears to be a type of wealth peculiar to capitalist societies. Material wealth of the individual owners originates out of their trading activities. The chief index of this type of wealth is in the form of firearms. During the centuries of the slaving operations it was indeed those Africans who specialized in supplying slaves to the Europeans who were the owners of the weapons. A crucial point about this type of wealth is that they were owned by merchants and traders. Another important point is that the wealth was not produced domestically but was the end result of trading activities, rather than the object of domestic External Labor.

A cross-sectional view of this vast continent at the middle of the fifteenth century would show a panorama of different peoples – communal hunter-gatherer-fisher; slave, slavemaster; landlord, landless peasant; landlord, landless peasant, merchant. They hunted and fished and gathered fruit. They maintained animal herds. They roamed a well-defined territorial complex to feed their animals as well as themselves. They traversed a wide area in order to cultivate the land under many methods of crop rotation and fallows. They cultivated orchards, raised animals, and husbanded the soil in sedentary communities. They grew food crops such as maize, rice, roots, plantains, ground nuts, legumes, bulbs, fruits. They grew fibers such as cotton, indigo, tobacco. They gathered forestry products such as dyewoods, gum, palm oil, timber. They cured the skins of animals such as sheep, goat, cattle.

They even mined the earth for iron ore, gold, salt, copper, tin, silver. They manufactured pig iron, charcoal, textile, leather goods, metal workings, soft drinks, beer.

Among themselves within a particular geographical domain, they bartered cloth, dyes, animals, slaves. In some cases they used rudimentary money in the form of cowries, iron bars, salt, cloth, copper rods. With the outside world some of them carried on a long-distance trade with the Atlantic islands as well as with faraway places across the Sahara Desert or down the lengths of the Nile. Some of the elements of this trade were gold, slaves, and ivory which flowed out of the domestic economies; horses, firearms and trinkets flowed in the opposite direction.

These facts would indicate that there were probably all three types of pre-capitalist societies in Africa at the middle of the fifteenth century. The exact number and their distribution among the three types of political economies is not known. However, we may still tentatively conclude that the most domineering type in wealth and power, if not in number of cases, was the highly developed feudal society. This type seems to be precisely the one which played the leading role in interactions with the Europeans as partners in the slave raiding and trading. The merchants of these societies, in consort with the ruling landed royalty, conquered the people of other societies and sold them as slaves to the Europeans.

The essential difference between these societies and the European societies of the same period seems to be that the class of merchants and traders in Africa received their biggest stimulus to growth and development in dealing in human flesh. The European merchants, while also the other partners in the human flesh exchange relations, supplied non-human material commodities which originated out of their own domestic production. Thus, their materials of exchange had a basis in capitalist production at home; the trade forged an intermediary link in the process of capital accumulation in the European economies. For the African merchants and landed royalty the exchange resulted in more ostentatious consumption.

In trying to assess the successful European onslaught against the

African societies we need to consider the other, lesser developed, feudal, slave, and communal societies which provided the fodder for slave hunting. We would think that the communal societies must have been the most vulnerable prey. We argued earlier that the inherent contradiction of the communal society must come from outside its geographical domain. It is the aliens who impose superior force of arms to disturb the tranquil domestic order.

Since European slaving ventures were so universal throughout Africa, we assume that domestic slave societies must have also fallen victim when the communal people were wiped out. Their vulnerability probably stemmed from the lack of arms to match the European guns.

Finally, internecine warfare among the powerful feudal states may even have taken its toll in slaves from these principalities.

The thesis is that the middle of the fifteen century was beset with a set of historical circumstances which brought about a confluence of forces in conspiracy to destroy simultaneously many of the existing communal, slave, and feudal societies in Africa. Since we know that the inherent contradictions of the latter two types stem from the dialectics of wealth in those societies, we venture the speculation that a good number of these societies were at a high stage of development in their historical epoch and were in relatively close transition to the next historical phase.

In the slave and feudal societies it is the extent of the intensity of External and Internal Labors, struggling against the ever increasing pressures of slave masters' or feudal landlords' personal force, that makes for the demise of the systems. The staggering material wealth of the ruling classes in these societies is a symptom of the crises.

At this time the continent was in ferment. The fermentation, no doubt, was accelerated by the intervention of the Europeans and their newfangled weaponry at the opportune time. At the same time, the African ruling classes helped to preside over the general malaise. We would like to believe that the powerful rulers of the huge feudal empires and their lesser vassals, ably assisted by a rising merchant class, were the most domineering agents of the whole sordid mess.

In the meantime, the lives of members of the laboring classes in all the various systems of political economies which prevailed must have been very precarious. Enslavement within one of the domestic economies, marching to the coast in chains for delivery to the

African origins of black Americans

European slave ships, providing military service as tribute to a feudal overlord in the capture and kidnapping of neighbors, tilling the soil under extreme conditions of labor for a master or landlord, building monuments to the afterlife of a king, seeing one's family succumb to the slaver's guns – all of these conditions must have made for great personal suffering and anxiety among the populations of workers throughout the length and breadth of the African lands.

The ultimate fate of the African was to be sealed in faraway places, in a strange clime, across the ocean. No matter what historical epoch they came out of in their native domains, they were to enter the crucible of slavery in the holds of alien ships, to start the process of being forged into a new population of slaves. All the different Africans would become one black people, trudging a new path of historical development, commencing in slavery, making its passage through the feudal epoch, and ending in modern-day wage laboring in an alien geographic domain within the most powerful capitalist nation the world has ever known.

We now turn to a consideration of the first phase in this new existence of black Americans.

5 The system of black slave labor and the rise of capitalism in Western Europe, 1619–1865

(The sordid enterprise of hunting black skins in Africa was an essential part of the commercial system that played a most important role in bringing about the demise of feudalism in Western Europe.) This same system of commerce – which embodied legitimate barter of material goods, deliberate looting, inhuman plunder, and unprecedented genocide – was to amass that necessary initial stock of capital wealth that would ultimately give birth to the new social epoch known as capitalism.

Commercial supremacy was the monopoly of the states of the Iberian peninsula in the beginning. In the middle of the fifteenth century, the mariners of Spain and Portugal made use of new sailing skills to successfully negotiate for the first time the northward return trip along the coastal waters of Africa, plying their vessels against the prevailing winds.

Thus began a series of events that would uproot the native people of the African continent, transport them across the Atlantic ocean, deposit them at coastal locations in South, Central, and North America, as well as in the islands of the Caribbean Sea. The bodies and blood of countless millions of African men, women, and children were ground into these foreign geographic domains through the instrumentalities of death and birth and death again from excruciating slave labor. Thus, came into existence the revitalized soils of the "new world."

For the next four centuries these strange involuntary migrants extended the process of Africanization of the American soil beyond the coastal areas to blanket the entire continents and islands. But the process of formation was under the control of the Western European marauders. At the same time, the great and glorious native peoples of these American lands were entombed in mines, put to death by the slaughterers' swords, and violently raped by the vicious swashbuckling conquistadores. In the meantime, the lucky survivors among them stood in mute witness to their ancient treasures of ancestral god-origins being looted and shipped off to Europe to form the private wealth of members of an established class of landed gentry and a rising class of merchants.

In time the Netherlands, Britain, France, Denmark, and Sweden joined the Iberian pirates in these machinations. The internecine struggles among these nations for control of the spoils ultimately resulted in the delineation of separate spheres of influence. After the conquest of Spain near the end of the sixteenth century, the English generally became lords and masters over the sugar and spice islands of the Caribbean and the tobacco colonies of North America.

The seventeenth century was indeed an age of revolution in British social and political organization. At the start, absolute monarchy ruled with an iron hand under a coalition with members of the landed aristocracy. By the end of the century, a new class of merchants and manufacturers had captured control of the political state and ruled from a posture of parliamentary power. The kings became relics of a bygone age, now playing the role of mere symbols of unity of the English people. The basis of economic power of the new ruling class partly arose out of the slave operations in Africa and the exploitation of slaves in the North American colonies for almost two centuries.

By the end of the eighteenth century, the British were expelled from their black slave colonies and an independent nation called the United States was formally proclaimed in North America. From then on, the saga of black Americans continued apace under some rather special conditions.

Atlantic slave operations as major source of capital accumulation in Western Europe, 1450–1790

A voluminous literature on the Atlantic slave trade exists. Most of it fails to document the importance of the relationship between the stock of capital that launched the system of capitalism in the world, on the one hand, and the overwhelming importance of the hunting

Black slave labor and the rise of capitalism

of black skins in Africa, their eventual sale in America, and the exploitation of their slave labor in the colonies on the other. Other factors in the development of European capitalism have been considered to be more important.

Capitalism requires for its existence, among other things, a class of capitalists and a class of wage laborers. Each member of the class of capitalists must privately own a quantum or more of capital; each member of the wage laboring class must be a private owner of her/his ability to work. At the same time the laborer must be devoid of ownership of the material means of survival. That is to say, the laborer must be personally free; but she/he must also be free from possession of her/his elementary food supply as well as of the material means of producing that food supply. The act of setting the European peasants free from feudal impoundment upon the manorial lands served this purpose well.

In the existing literature some of the historical methods by which wage laborers and capitalists came into existence are said to be the robbery of common peasant lands and church estates, the land enclosures for grazing sheep, the expulsion of the peasants from the land, the use of the political state under a mercantilist policy to protect trade monopolies and to foster the development of new manufacturing industry. Only a few works have taken on the task of demonstrating the leading role of the slave trade and the ensuing exploitation of slave labor.

The complex set of activities involved in the European slaving operations can be best understood in the context of capitalist industry functioning in a special sector of European capitalist External Labor Processes. This sector required both the material means and the subjective element of External Labor. More specifically, the sector required a minimal stock of capital, distributed in planned proportions among such things as equipment (outfitted ships, port facilities in both Europe and Africa, warehouses in Europe, prisons in Africa); raw materials (textiles, guns, gunpowder, iron bars, copper bars, alcoholic beverages, tobacco, pottery, trinkets, ship's stores); and money.

The money was partly used to purchase the human energies of the ships' operating crews, military personnel, and other supporting gangs.

The specific External Labor activities consisted of organizing and managing the personnel; loading the outfitted ships with the raw

Black slave labor and the rise of capitalism

materials and ships' stores; undertaking the sea voyage to Africa; hunting and trading for black slaves in Africa; providing for temporary imprisonment of the slaves at the African ports; undertaking the sea voyage across the Atlantic to the Americas; preparing the slaves for display to prospective buyers; consummating the actual sales of the slaves for gold or other suitable monetary material; and undertaking the return voyage to the European ports, sailing empty. Although ships may transport materials to Europe on the return voyage, such activity is to be considered as part of a separate, but related, enterprise.

Finally, the process is completed when the empty ships, in the European ports, are augmented in numbers, properly outfitted, reloaded with the necessary complement of crews and raw materials, and take leave of Europe for another round of slaving in Africa. (The expanded operation in the current round was made possible by using the profits of the previous venture to replace used up raw materials and equipment, to invest in net additions to these ingredients, and to increase, if necessary, the slaving personnel. Such investments of the profits represented the specific form in which capital was accumulated within the slaving sector of British and other European economies.)

(The first thing to observe is that the operational aspects of the sector occurred primarily outside Europe; at the same time, however, the capital accumulation aspects of the sector are carried out primarily inside Europe. A second important observation is that the activity did not involve the production of consumer commodities for sale in a domestic market; it was essentially the transformation of domestically produced raw materials and equipment into foreign gold. Slaves were the intermediary product; they were produced outside the domestic European economies and effectively "exported" in exchange for money capital which flowed back to Europe from abroad. The mercantilist phase of capitalist development could thus thrive in perfect harmony with the theoretical basis for its justification.\

The slaving sector served a host of other sectors throughout the European economies. It enabled the equipment and raw material manufacturers to convert their gross profits into money. Some industries – shipbuilding, construction, ordnance, textiles, banking, insurance, iron, alcoholic beverage manufacture – were the direct and immediate beneficiaries. Other industries benefited indirectly

Black slave labor and the rise of capitalism

from dealings with the immediate suppliers of the slaving sector. In addition, there were the impacts on the development of a consumer commodity market from the ultimate purchases of the ships' crews and other personnel.

Over the course of the four centuries of slaving, one can identify various alternative measures of its impact on European capitalist development. The most direct measure, however, is the quantity of the specific product of these operations. The number of slaves captured and brought to the Americas is the most direct and significant measure of the contribution. Nowhere in the literature is this fact well understood. As a matter of fact, there seems to be a deliberate conspiracy among certain scholars periodically to conduct rather spurious "censuses" which systematically pare away at the number of Africans involved in this sordid business.

In principle, problems of estimating the numbers are not too difficult to solve, provided we make use of a few simple truisms and invoke some assumptions implicit in the arguments of Chapters 1 and 2.

Consider any arbitrary period consisting of a continuous span of one hundred years. Call this period the "population formation period" or simply the "current period." Call the first year of the current period the "initial year." Finally, call the last year of the period the "current year."

Now, every living member of the population during the current year is a surviving residue of foreign birth or of native birth which took place during the current period. On the other hand, those who died during the current period include some who were born prior to the current period, and therefore were alive at the beginning of the initial year. The remaining deaths during the current period include some who were born within the domestic economy and some who were born abroad.

On our theory the result of the operations of the Internal Labor Process is to produce the potential population. This consists of all those who were alive within the domestic economy at the beginning of the initial year, all migrants into the domestic economy from abroad during the current period, and all native births during the current period.

During the current year, the survivors from domestic births must replace the initial population as well as the non-surviving migrants who entered the domestic economy during the current period.

Black slave labor and the rise of capitalism

During the current year, the survivors from domestic births may even contribute an "increment" to the current year survivors over the initial year survivors.

In this work we shall assume that the slave society generates zero growth out of domestic births; that is to say, the contribution of domestic births to an increment in the current year survivors over the initial year survivors is zero. It follows that total domestic births during the current period equals total deaths during that same period.

A very important implication flowing from these facts and assumptions is that the surviving population in the current year is numerically equal to the total import of slaves over the entire history of the slave society. The actual surviving members of such a slave population during the current year will be distributed among both native born and imports; the native born will be concentrated among the younger members of the survivors, while the imports will be dominant among the older surviving members.

This model of slave reproduction is quite intriguing. It gives us a simple way of estimating the number who came from abroad. It also tells us something about the nature of the slave Internal Labor Process. Births in such a society respond in such a way as to just offset the ravages of death from slave External Labor during the current period. Thus, any expansion in numbers of slave survivors over the long haul must rely on a continuing and uninterrupted importation of human flesh from outside the domestic economy. The actual persistence of the Atlantic "slave trade" over the centuries is thus seen to be not an anomaly, but an endemic characteristic of British North American colonial slavery.

The first US Census of population placed the number of blacks at 760,000 in 1790. This gives us a first approximation of the number of slave imports into the colonies from the first influx in 1619 to the end of the colonial era. This number is the true and direct impact of the so-called Atlantic slave trade on the development of capitalism in Great Britain. When translated in terms of the then contemporary British economy, the impact should be staggering indeed.

We need not go to the records to determine what the slaves were actually sold for. The "real" value is invariant with time. It is the number of human life-years congealed in more than three quarters of a million live bodies. To fix ideas, let us assume an average age of that surviving population of, say, fifteen years. This would calculate to the equivalent of approximately eleven and one-half million life years. We need not go much beyond this to identify a major source of the primitive capital that launched the British into the capitalist epoch during the seventeenth and eighteenth centuries, as a consequence of just the slave "trade" alone, and the resulting payments in gold and silver and other precious metals for eleven and one-half million life-years of living black human flesh.

The gold and other precious metals that flowed back to the mother country in payment for the black human flesh was no ordinary commodity. Indeed, we must recall that in capitalist society profits first come into existence for each individual capitalist in the form of the specific commodity which he causes to be produced. That is to say, the initial profit is the total quantity of the commodity produced, minus that portion which represents the value of the wages paid to the laborers who produced it.

But capitalists are not in the business of accumulating capital in the form of their own inventories. Commodities are produced to be sold. Hence, the second form in which profits must occur is in the form of the money commodity. This means that the initial form of profits must be converted into money if the capitalist cycle of profit-making is to succeed.

Finally, no individual capitalist is worth his salt unless he can repeat the cycle of production of commodities, sale of commodities, and accumulation of money capital all over again during the following period. This means that he must take the entire monetary proceeds from the sale of his commodity and use these proceeds to replace used up equipment and raw materials as well as to purchase additional increments of these types of capital; replace the wages paid out to his workers; add to his inventory; and most significantly of all end up with an increment to his money holdings.

This detailed recitation is important in understanding the role of the slave "trade" on the British domestic economy. The slaves represented "intermediary" gold. Actual gold flowed back into the coffers of the slavers. They in turn had to use it to capitalize their gross profits. That is to say, in the replacement and additions to their raw materials and equipment they were also providing the monetary basis for the capitalization of the profits of their direct suppliers of these commodities. In turn their direct suppliers were provided the monetary base for the conversion of profits into money of the secondary suppliers to the slaving industry, and so on *ad infinitum*.

In the early phase of capitalist economy the physical money metal plays a decisive role. It cannot be dispensed with; nor can the complex financial institutions for manipulating the money supply that we know in the modern world be brought into play at this juncture. Thus, the slaving operations were the central engine that drove British capitalist development with an impact far beyond its monetary magnitude. The qualitative role in providing the canonical form of capital was unmatched by any other sector of British industry, or by any other social forces involved in the development of capitalism.

Placed in the context of all the events which were contributing to the transformation of the feudal English countryside into a capitalist economy, slaving obviously played a second place to no other influence. In the rather harsh appraisal of Marx, "the treasures captured outside Europe by undisguised looting, enslavement, and murder, floated back to the mother-country and were there turned into capital."

Simultaneous with the slaving operations in Africa and across the Atlantic was the establishment of the colonies in North America in which black slave labor was exploited for the benefit of the various sponsors of the colonial ventures. Naturally, the colonial enterprises were established by the British for private profit in the same way as they established any other capitalist enterprise in Britain. Nevertheless, within the colonies themselves the conditions of reproduction of the slave population were based on slave society relations, not capitalist reproductive relations. At the same time that the system of slavery functioned in the colonies as a *bona fide* slave society, essential connecting conduits, however, were put into place to siphon off the material wealth produced by the slaves into the private coffers of the capitalist corporations (joint stock companies) and individuals who were the authors of the colonial schemes. In short, the slave society in the colonies was riveted in a specific way to serve the wealth accumulation requirements of the capitalist social system in the mother-country, over and beyond the spoils garnered from the slave "trade."

Two distinct phases of black slavery in North America must be distinguished. The first was the colonial era under British dominion, and ending with the founding of an independent United

States. The second followed on the successful completion of the American War of National Liberation and ended with the so-called American Civil War. In both cases, however, it is unrecompensed black American slave labor that was transformed into material wealth of others.

Reproduction of the black American slave political economy

Coincident with the Atlantic slave trade, the maritime nations of Western Europe wasted no time in establishing colonies throughout the Americas based on black slave labor. The Portuguese and Spanish were notorious for their rapacious quests for gold and other precious metals. As a spin-off they at times settled for second-best. Dye woods from Brazil, spices from the Caribbean, elixir of youth from Florida, and sugar from Santo Domingo were all important material bounties from the American ventures. Nevertheless, these two countries were more noted for their inhuman murders and lootings of the ancient treasures of the native people with whom they came in contact.

The British, French, and Dutch concentrated on the establishment of sugar colonies in the Caribbean. Their greed for gold and precious metals was partly satisfied by piratical raids on Spanish and Portuguese galleons. Moreover, the British were also quite devious in wresting from the Spanish the right to even supply the Spanish colonies with black African slaves. Another source of the yellow metal was thus secured.

Of immediate interest to us was the establishment of the settler colonies in North America by the British. The sponsors represented the capitalist class, either as individuals or as members of corporations, in league with the royal family and its allies among the landed gentry. The colonies were designed as profit-making capitalist ventures, based on the ceding of land by the Crown to certain individuals or corporations in exchange for annual monetary payments, tributes in kind, and other forms of bounty.

The leaders of the settlements relied on various techniques for inducing English common folk to come to live in the colonies. A good number of these were kidnapped, forced to come from debtor's prisons on pain of remaining there forever, or induced to seek religious and other freedoms not effectively available in the mother-country.

Most of these "free" people were made to work as indentured servants for various periods of years before they could be free to pursue their own activities. Working the land under this type of tenure arrangement was tantamount to feudal relations. And so many colonies were established, one of the most famous and successful being the settlement at Jamestown in 1607. Other settlements in New England, New York, Pennsylvania, Maryland, Virginia, the Carolinas, and Georgia soon set the basis for a colonial mode of exploitation. But much more was at stake in this burgeoning North American domain.

An essential ingredient in practically all of these colonies was the organization of a black slave-labor-based economy. The material form of wealth in these colonies was the living slaves, owned as private property of members of the slave-owning class.

The first black slaves presumably were introduced into Jamestown in 1619. Between 1619 and 1790 an estimated 760,000 had been shipped directly or indirectly from Africa to the British North American colonies. This represented an average annual import of slaves of 4,500 over the one hundred and seventy-one year period.

The first slave masters originated with the establishment of the colonies. Private corporations and individuals received monopoly charters to own and exploit specific geographic areas in the Americas. Some of these individuals actually took up settlement, bringing with them common folk to work the land under conditions of indentured servitude. Other individuals and corporations made grants of land to any settler who brought indentured servants to the new world. The size of the land grant depended upon the number of such servants brought over.

In any case, the sponsors of the colonies were in the operations for a profit. They imposed conditions under which the settlers would pay them tributes in kind of the products produced, taxes, duties, and other bounties. The so-called Crown also figured among the colonial sponsors, making it possible for members of the royal families and their aristocratic allies to profit from these ventures. In time, the Crown was to take over the general defense and management of all the colonies. Nevertheless, even under this latter arrangement private profitability of the British investors was assured.

Black slave labor and the rise of capitalism

The two distribution processes that bound the black slaves to their material means of survival resided in the personal will of each slave master. The slave master personally dictated that every slave man, woman, and child must participate in the External Labor Process. This same slave master personally dictated the quantity of the material means of survival that each slave would receive to carry out the activities of Internal Labor.

The constant threats of punishment and death, the ever-present firearms on the side of the master, the awesome presence of armed overseers, the constant whippings, the physical maimings, the rape of slave women, the withholding of the most elementary privileges, the denials of any formal education, the controlled religious ceremonies, the breaking up of slave families for sale to other slave masters — all of these are examples of the visible indices of the personal force exerted on the slaves to keep them within the slave property relations.

On the other hand, an equal and counter-balancing set of forces was continuously exerted by the slaves. The struggles of the slaves for survival, for liberation from the shackles of slave master private property aggrandizement, were continuously manifested in the alternating phases of slave External and slave Internal Labor. The transformation of the population of slaves into tobacco and other material products, followed by the transformation of the slave food rations into slaves, carried on in alternating sequence over time, were the dramatic moments of the struggle for survival in the prosecution of the two phases of slave labor.

So long as the countervailing forces of private property in ownership of slaves was in dynamic balance with the forces unleashed by slave labor, the slave system functioned as if the slaves were in complete acquiescence to their lot. In the words of the neo-classical economists, the system was in equilibrium. Only when violent incidents of slave revolt ensued, or only when unusually harsh punishment was inflicted on a particular slave did it become evident that the opposing forces were in active and continuing conflict. Equilibrium on the surface only concealed churning volcanic fires smoldering at the core of the system of black human slavery.

The slave External Labor Process was under the complete ownership and control of the slave master. He personally decided what materials were to be produced, in what quantity, and by what technique of production. Thus, the slave master dictated the duration and intensity of the slave's External Labor. Since no costs were incurred by the slave master, the volume of material production, or the revenue derived therefrom, was the relevant variable to be maximized. This could obviously be accomplished, if necessary, by pushing the labor of the slaves to its outer limits of duration and intensity. Extremely hard labor from sun-up to sun-down, under the watchful eye of the overseer, could well characterize this process in the real world.

In the British colonial era, tobacco was the main product of slave External Labor. Sugar, rice, indigo, hemp also played important roles. All products were produced primarily for export outside the slave system, mostly to Great Britain for its own use or for re-export to other European countries.

The Internal Labor Process was also under the complete control and ownership of the slave master. He dictated the type and quantity of population to be produced and the technique of production. Thus, the slave master also dictated the intensity and duration of slave Internal Labor. If the ravages of External Labor killed off too many, or if the demands of an expanding geographic domain required an unusual increase in the number of slaves, the duration and intensity of slave Internal Labor could be pushed to the limits of intensity and duration. A stepping up of the intensification of slave baby-producing activity from sun-down to sun-up, fueled by high caloric foods in just the right quantities, could be a vehicle for such contingencies in the real world.

Wealth in this society was accumulated by the slave master in the material form of the living slaves. The process of accumulation was accomplished by binding the entire slave population with part of the food produced, directly or indirectly, by the slaves. Such a bond, of course, was nothing more or less than the population of living slaves, cemented in a joint producing and consuming mode, under the private ownership of the slave master. That is to say, both elements – slave population and their food supply – of the synthesis, as well as the resulting material products – reproduced slave population, reproduced food supply, tobacco – were the private property of the slave master and not of the slaves. But this wasn't the end of the accumulation process.

The remainder of the newly produced food was consumed by the slave master for his own personal reproduction. The tobacco, cotton, indigo, rice, hemp, were exported for cash; in turn the cash was converted to paying taxes, bounties, commissions, interest; the remainder was converted into luxury consumption of the master of such items as Romanesque mansions, fancy clothing, lavish entertaining, proper education for the master's children, gaudy monuments, and other exhibitions of power and influence.

The entire material product of slave External Labor was thus expropriated by the slave master. Part was consumed by the master and part was consumed by the slave population. The latter part reproduced the existing slave population; the former part, not returned to slave Internal Labor, represented the killing off of the newly created slave population. Hence, slave wealth accumulation tends to remain unchanged over time.

This dynamic of slave wealth accumulation is absent from the literature on slavery. It suggests that, at least for a significant period of time, a slave political economy is beset with the contradiction that its material form of wealth is the living slaves, yet it kills them off in the reproductive process.

The unbounded greed for revenues to satiate the personal appetites of the slave masters, however, generates the necessity for expansion of the living slave population. This can only be accomplished by resorting to a system of importation of new slave bodies from abroad. But the stepping up in the level of imports generates a corresponding increase in the number of deaths among these imports within the domestic economy; a stepping up in the deaths of the imports within the domestic economy calls forth a corresponding increase in the number of native births to offset such deaths. In time, the intensity of slave Internal Labor reaches a critical level which causes an acceleration in the number of slave births from one current period to the next. When these conditions occur, the system of slave labor enters a new phase in its historical development.

The visible result of this wealth accumulation dynamic was a surviving population composed of about 70 per cent native-born slaves and 30 per cent foreign-born slaves, the sum total of both equal in number and even age distribution to the total past imports of slaves from abroad.

When the total surviving population reaches a certain critical mass slave reproduction autonomously generates a growing population independent of imports. This latter condition seemed to have been at least partly in place by the end of the colonial era.

Black slave labor and the rise of capitalism

We cannot leave the British colonial slave era without pausing to reiterate the extent of exploitation of slave labor during the 171 years of its existence. The most direct measure of such exploitation is either the extent of slave External Labor or slave Internal Labor.

The literature abounds with estimates of the physical quantity of tobacco and other material products of slave labor during this era. One alternative and equivalent measure, however, is the extent of slave Internal Labor, represented materially by the sum total of live slave births produced domestically.

The Political State under slavery was conditioned by the fact that during the colonial period it operated under general British legal rule, in conjunction with other colonies that were not strictly speaking slave colonies.

During the last population formation period under colonial slavery we estimate that 1,113,000 black slaves were born within the domestic economy. An estimated equal number also died within the domestic economy during the same period. This number, and the implications it has for the corresponding production of material goods in the slave External Labor Process, are a true measure of British expropriation of slave wealth during the colonial era.

After independence, the system of slavery won a very powerful, if not equal, partnership in the coalition government of national liberation. The slave system was able to circumscribe the national coalition government's powers to interfere with the relatively autonomous slave states and the rights of some of the nationals within these states to exploit black human slave labor as their own private property. Within the states, moreover, a complex of local governments handled the day-to-day tasks of police functions peculiar to their own circumstances.

Since each slave plantation was ruled with personal force of the slave master, and since very little interdependence existed among the slave owners, political power was obviously distributed in proportion to the number of slaves owned.

Government bureaucracies at all levels, ably assisted by "free" white peasants, and in conjunction with a host of supporting social institutions, worked hand in glove to provide the context and controlling mechanisms for the legitimate exercise of slave state power by the slave owners. Legislative acts, local customs and practices, the religious incantations, education, the arts, the literature, the intellectual rationalizations, interpretations of the organic law of the land and of the bill of rights – all of these came together in conspiratorial alliances to support and maintain a system of exploitation of black human bodies and blood and will and aspirations for life.

The brutality of this system which made material poverty the lot of the producers of wealth and which simultaneously made the parasites materially wealthy was to meet its doom. The greed of its ruling class, seeking out to aggrandize its wealth upon the backs of the black slaves in consort with the outside world, trading slave-produced materials to sate its vicious appetites, would bring into revolutionary play a set of contradictions of the system of slavery.

Freedom was proclaimed in the nation. Yet we must not lose sight of the fact that more than 20 per cent of the nation's population, and probably half of the south's population, remained the private property of other human beings.

Black slave labor as source of primitive capital accumulation in the United States, 1790–1865

The system of slavery as practiced in America is generally analyzed in terms of its moral incompatibility with the laws of human conduct; or in terms of the vicious practice of white racism; or in terms of the peculiar way of life of a region gone half mad; or in terms of many other similar characteristics.

The brute fact, however, is that slavery in America was a specific form of exploitation of human labor, a distinct mode of human social organization. It was by no means unique to America nor to the real time period in which it occurred there. It stands as one of the three great types of exploiting societies in the history of humankind. Practically every nation today has undergone this special phase in its historical development at some time in the past.

In the United States, however, the system of slavery had the peculiar distinction that the slaves were all black. More specifically, they were black Africans who were uprooted from their native habitats and transported across the Atlantic Ocean as the objects of capitalistic ventures undertaken by European merchant capitalists. Because the slaves were sold in European settled colonies in America, their masters were non-black. Thus, there came into being the confluence of what appears on the surface to be racist events – white slave masters of black slaves.

(We must not forget the important fact that within the system of slavery in the United States a rather large class of white landless peasants and white subsistence farmers played a significant role. These whites had no power to exploit black slave labor. Although they were the human instruments by which the ruling slaveocracy kept the black slaves in check, they nevertheless could not exploit slave labor for their private benefits. They should therefore be distinguished from the white slave master class.)

Race relations, then, can only be viewed in terms of master-slave interactions, a set of interactions in which a relatively small group of white masters accumulated black slaves as private wealth and exploited their labor for personal revenues. Over the period from 1790 to 1865 the extent of exploitation of black slave labor by the relatively few white slave masters was total. During this period the surviving black population increased from 760,000 to almost 5,000,000, an annual gain of more than 50,000. This is an awesome number.

If importation of slaves during this period were negligible, as the literature generally implies, then the slave regime would have had to intensify the slave Internal Labor to the unprecedented extent of creating almost ten million slave births over the seventy-five year period. Slave births would have had to exceed 130,000 annually.

We do not believe that such a model accurately depicts slave Internal Labor. We acknowledge that this period represented a transitional period, the last phase in the slave society's existence. Therefore, a departure from the colonial slave Internal Labor Process is entirely possible. But we cannot believe that slave imports could have disappeared with such finality.

If imports continued at an average of 4,600 per year, total slave births over the period 1790 to 1865 would total 7,400,000 for an average of almost 100,000 annually.

The end of colonialism removed one layer of exploitation from the backs of the slaves. This alone could have caused a reduction in the rate, if not in the absolute level, of slave exploitation. The immediate result of such an event would be an increase in the surviving slave population out of domestic births. This in turn could have stimulated an increment in births during one year over the preceding year. Such an increment of approximately 3,000 births could account for the drastic change in the surviving population during the period of US slavery.

The period of transition of the slave epoch to some other form of social organization could have also played a part in the observed survival pattern. Southern slavery was becoming more and more interdependent with the developing capitalist economy outside of the south. This new entanglement in the web of capitalist machinations would set in place the mechanisms by which some of the cotton and other material goods produced by slave labor flowed into the coffers of people outside of the slave domain and were there transformed into capital. In time that capital would launch the beginnings of what was to emerge as the most powerful capitalist nation the world has ever known.

It must be recalled that the most elementary, and therefore the most important, material form of wealth in slave society is the slave. At the demise of the slave system in 1865 this wealth existed in the form of approximately five million blacks. This number, however, was the surviving residue of more than eight million black live births over the previous 75-year period.

These eight million black slave births represent the material form of the Internal Labor generated by the black slaves to ensure their survival during the year 1865. It is therefore an exact measure of the External Labor exerted by black slaves to produce all of the cotton and other material goods for slave masters during 1865. Each of these magnitudes, of opposite and equal labor, measures the real reproducible wealth of the class of slave owners just before their exploiting system collapsed forever.

Part of the goods created through exploitation of black slave labor found its way into northern textile mills. Cotton and other slave-produced goods were marketed for cash sales in New York, Boston, New Orleans, and other centers. Typically, an agent would be entrusted with marketing activities – securing credit from local banks during the growing season; selling the cotton to intermediate or final users outside the slave south; using the cash proceeds to pay off principal and interest on the loans, pay for foreign and domestic goods for slave master personal consumption, pay his own commission. Already we encounter a series of parasites – local banks, local and other warehousemen and shippers, northern textile industry, northern and foreign exporters of luxury consumables, etc.

It must be emphasized that from the perspective of the slave system, cotton was not a *bona fide* commodity. It was not produced by wage laborers; nor did it encounter any costs of production. To the slave masters, therefore, any so-called price greater than zero would be acceptable. The volume of consumables that could be bought with the sale proceeds was the controlling variable; it would increase any time that the unit price of cotton did not yield a revenue consistent with the style to which the slave masters had become accustomed. But such revenues could increase only with increased exertion of slave labor. Thus, if market prices fell, then intensification of slave labor proceeded in the opposite direction.

The ultimate users of the cotton were capitalists who must have had the upper hand in the quasi-market transactions with slave owners. They could exact relatively cheap prices inasmuch as the cotton had no alternative use to the slave owners. Cheaper prices meant bigger profits. But in addition, to the extent that cotton clothing entered into the real wage of the textile and other workers, the effects on profits would be enhanced.

In due time the exploitation of the slave labor became more and more interfaced with the demands of the outside world. Northern capitalist demand for slave-produced cotton and other goods, the corresponding demand for northern goods to satisfy slave master consumption needs, the corresponding exertion of slave labor to the outer limits of endurance, the achievement of conditions under which slave reproduction yielded net additions independent of slave imports, the corresponding pressures for extension of slave geographic territory – all these and many more related influences came together to hasten the development as well as the demise of the slave system.

By 1861 these forces manifested themselves in a series of social explosions, ultimately ending in the so-called War Between the States.

6 The black sharecropping system and the development of capitalism in the United States, 1865–1965

(The black sharecropping labor system came into being shortly after the end of the so-called Civil War. It was a special type of exploitative labor system, based on feudal property relations which bound the newly freed slaves to the land under the control of a class of landowners. This system was a natural evolutionary successor to the former slave labor system which had prevailed for almost 250 years.)

At the time of its demise black slavery had achieved its highest development. Slave Internal and External Labor had been pushed to their utmost level of intensity, such that a relatively rapid net reproduction of the slave population was proceeding apace independently of the necessity for importation of human flesh from abroad.

From some three-quarters of a million living slaves at the founding of the nation, this slave population had approached nearly five million survivors by the end of the Civil War. Perhaps about one hundred thousand annual live births were necessary to sustain such growth.

These numbers congeal the quantity of slave owners' wealth in living human flesh. The corresponding material goods consumed or consumable by the slave owners, or shared with the retinue of intermediary parasites outside the slave south, were also part of the slave owners' wealth.

Other indicators of the development of slavery were the projected expansion of slave territory in the west as well as into Mexico, Central America, and the Caribbean; and slave owners' exercise of a not inconsiderable degree of control over some of the major organs of national state power, including the armed force.

These and other factors were beginning to solidify the outside opposition.

Members of the northern capitalist class, independent northern and western farmers, farm laborers, tenants, and wage laborers were being roped in as natural allies against the slaveocrats. Not to be ignored was the black slave – the most natural enemy of the slave masters – who formed an essential element of this alliance.

The small band of slaveocrats railroaded the southern independent farmers, farm laborers, and mountain whites into an uneasy alliance against the opposition. It was remarkable indeed that they could get the support of a group of people whom they had heretofore treated with disdain and whom they had used as unofficial police forces to carry out their dirty work.

The immediate catalysts for the conflict were the issues involved in the secession of the slave states from the national political state and from the corresponding reaction of the northern capitalists to preserve the coalition government which was forged during the war of liberation from Great Britain. In truth, the real cause was a usurpation by northern capitalists of national state power, which was being wielded primarily in their own interests. Correspondingly, the slaveocracy withdrew from the coalition to organize its own independent political state, over which it could exercise unchallenged authority within its own slave domain. These conflicts obviously commenced long before 1861.

The use of state power by northern capitalists to speed up the development of industry encompassed many of the underlying bases of the conflict. Tariff and other measures to protect manufacturing industry from foreign competition, federal land policy and other acts which fostered the rapid development of a national transportation network (railroads, highways, canals), restrictions on the expansion of slavery into the new territories and states, outlawing of the Atlantic slave trade – all of these and many related issues defined the arena of conflict.

By means of military conquest and the assumption of political hegemony over the national political state, the northern capitalists were able to destroy the slaveocracy in one fell swoop. The revolutionary act was the freeing of the slaves. This single event smashed the economic power of the slave owners and thus destroyed them as a class in society. Their material basis of wealth now gone, this erstwhile class was reduced to the ashes of history. Never before in the history of the world had a revolution been so decisive. Not even the French Revolution could claim so unambiguous a victory.

A most important corollary of the freeing of the slaves was the simultaneous "freeing" up of the slaves' food supply. This fact has gone unnoticed and does not seem to be well understood or appreciated as a necessary condition for the development of capitalism on a national basis. Its decisive impact was on the development of a national domestic market system. It also had an important impact on the nature of the capital accumulation process itself.

While the freeing up of the slave food supplies was not a necessary condition for the establishment of a feudal system which came to the south, it was nevertheless an absolutely necessary condition for the development of capitalism on a national, rather than on a regional, basis. In this context it meant converting the former slaves' food supplies into commodities. That is to say, henceforth, food can only be acquired by the southern as well as non-southern working classes through the intermediation of money purchases on a market, and not by direct production by such working classes for their own personal consumption.

This conversion of food into a commodity also became a most powerful lever for establishing the essential linkages of the southern sharecropping system with the system of capitalist economy outside of the south. Hence, its role in the process of capital accumulation was assured.

This "food" question can explain the rapid decline in food self-sufficiency in the south as a whole. Corn, other grain, livestock herds all declined drastically after the war. The growing and inevitable dependence of both sharecropper and landlord on cash with which to purchase food and other consumables would explain the corresponding necessity of an ever-increasing devotion to the growing of a cash crop in cotton, rice, sugar, etc.

Thus, a merchant class was able to provide a direct conduit by which some of the surplus products of the sharecroppers' labor could be accumulated as capital in the northern banks and industries.

Capital soon began to appear in the north in the material form of cotton, as it were, dripping with the blood of the black cropper and his white counterpart. Economic development in the south was arrested for another century. The catchword would be "poverty among the southern producers of wealth; material riches among the few northern expropriators of that wealth."

The reproduction of the black sharecropping political economy

The basic form of wealth in this system was the material product of the cropper's labor on the land. Cotton reigned supreme during this era.

A very special working out of the wealth relations typified southern agriculture. The food which ended up in the stomachs of the cropper was owned by northern and western capitalists, and in part by local merchants. The southern landlords owned a good share of the immediate produce of the cropper's labor. A part of the cotton could be converted by the landlord indirectly into food through purchase or barter arrangements with the local merchants. A very small part of the cotton was owned by the cropper, who could also convert it into food by barter or purchase from the local merchant.

The social relations spawned by private ownership of wealth in the society were rather complex, involving the interlocking contacts between black sharecroppers, southern white landlords, northern and western capitalists, and local merchants. These classes constituted the human actors in the social drama. The implicit role and distinguishing characteristics of each were easily understood. It must be emphasized that it was the black sharecropper, the producer of all the material basis of wealth, who lay alone at the bottom of the economic heap.

Unlike the slave, however, the sharecropper was personally free. He could not be held as the private property of any other social class. The cropper originated out of the former slaves who had been freed as a consequence of the northern victory in the war. Except for a relatively few freedmen who were able to acquire some land, practically all the former slaves made up this class.

There was a significant number of white croppers. However, the black families were more concentrated in this class. White croppers did have some alternative to become wage laborers. On the other hand, blacks were practically without any other mode of survival.

The merchant class constituted another important class in the post-bellum south. This class was not necessary to the feudal relations which were established. Yet, the peculiar circumstances surrounding the demise of American slavery gave rise to this class. Its role was decisive in the process of accumulation of wealth produced by the sharecroppers.

The landlord class owned the direct and immediate produce of the sharecropper's labor upon the land. Some were the former slave owners or their heirs. A good many, however, came from a variety of sources. Theft, purchase, fraudulent acquisitions of private or public lands were some of the "idyllic" methods by which this class arose. This class should not be confused with the old slave master class. The conditions of their existence as a class are quite different from those of slave owners.

Both distribution processes operated always as a unity. Only a conceptual distinction separated them. A written contract was the instrument for distributing the sharecroppers to the tasks of producing cotton; this same instrument provided for the amount of cotton that would be returned to the croppers.

Under the contract the sharecropper agreed to work the land under the direction and control of the landlord. The crop that was to be produced (generally cotton) was stipulated, as well as the conditions under which the cropper would work and the aids to be provided by the landlord. A given quantity of land was provided by the landlord to be worked; tools, mules, seed, etc. were also provided in varying amounts among different landlords and croppers.

The same contract stipulated the amount of the produce of the sharecropper that would be turned over to the landlord; the remainder would become the property of the cropper. In general, the contracts specified a fifty-fifty percentage share arrangement. In practice, however, landlords were able to reduce the cropper's share down to the barest minimum level consistent with the reproductive food requirements of the cropper.

The contract had the sanction of law. If violated, the cropper could be brought to justice. This contract was also enforceable by specific and oppressive customs of the locality. There was no mystery why law and custom such as ku klux klan violence militated against the cropper and in favor of the landlord. Such a contract and the enforcement mechanisms were the specific instruments that riveted the cropper to the land under conditions subord-

Black sharecropping and capitalism in the US

inate to the landlord. It is also the same agreement which riveted the cropper and his family to a meager quantity of the material means of survival.

Although the stipulated period was generally one year, in practice these were lifetime contracts, renewable yearly at the discretion of the landlord. The land provided was of a size that the cropper and his family could reasonably till, with some sort of shack for living quarters.

The percentage sharing left enough incentive for the cropper to exert his External Labor to the maximum. Under these arrangements any increase in the absolute amount produced would yield the cropper an increase in the absolute share received. In spite of this, however, a noticeable effect of the introduction of this system was the apparent withdrawal of a significant amount of the External Labor time of the cropper's wife and children, as compared to the days of slavery.

The cropper had no choice as to what was to be produced. In general, he was forbidden to grow any food at all for his family's personal consumption. All of the time was to be devoted to the production of a stipulated cash crop. Pressures from the local merchants as well as the personal needs of the landlords made the cash nexus more and more necessary.

Since the crop was cotton or some other inedible material, it had to be at least partly converted into food and other consumables.

In the post-bellum south the class of merchants provided the intermediation to make the conversion of cotton into food possible. The merchant took complete charge of marketing the cotton crop. The specific procedure would be to provide food and other consumables to both the landlord and the cropper during the gestation period of the crop. The future crop and the land would be taken as collateral against such credit. At the end of the growing season the cotton would be turned over to the merchant, who in turn would market it, take out the proceeds for his credit, and turn the rest, if any, over to the landlord and cropper. In the meantime, the merchant would establish relations with local banks, northern banks, and wholesale establishments to replenish his stocks during the growing season. A link was thus established with the capitalist world outside of the sharecropping enclave in the south.

Theoretically, any amount of cash over and beyond the consumption requirements necessary to reproduce the landlord and the cropper would provide a basis for accumulation of wealth by these two classes. However, the cropper started out with a certain percentage of the yield of his labor. At this point he is at the mercy of the landlord in terms of a series of extra charges that must be deducted for a wide variety of reasons. Then he is at the mercy of the merchant's exorbitant prices and credit charges for the provisions which he had to consume during the year. In practice, the cropper was unable to accumulate any material wealth. He was, however, capable of reproducing himself and his family, and thus he partook in the reproduction of a sharecropping class readily available for exploitation by the other two classes in the southern enclave.

In so far as the landlord was not also a merchant, he too, was subject to the wiles of the merchant class and was generally unable to accumulate any significant material wealth other than durable consumables. In any case, members of this class were able to indulge significant personal consumption of both food and luxuries. As such, they were generally able to survive as landlords.

The entire surplus produced by the cropper found its way into two channels; one reproduced the landlord, the other went into the pocket of the merchant. The merchant's share in turn was not all the property of the merchant. Indeed, he had to distribute part of it to his own financial correspondent, local and northern banks, his northern suppliers of provisions on which his business rested, brokers, and manufacturers who ultimately purchased the cotton to fuel the textile industry in the north or abroad.

Northern capitalists throughout the various non-textile industries and capitalist growers of food in the west were also indirect beneficiaries. In so far as relatively cheap cotton helped to cheapen the clothing and other cotton goods purchased by non-south laborers, real wages of these workers were kept in check and thus contributed to capitalist profits far beyond the geographic boundaries of the sharecropping domain.

A measure of the amount of capital accumulated on the backs of the black croppers can be found in the value of all the cotton and other material goods produced by the croppers, minus the value of the food consumed by all the croppers. This is a measure of the results of cropper External Labor not returned to the sharecropping class.

An alternative measure could be sought in the results of cropper

Black sharecropping and capitalism in the US

Internal Labor not showing up in the surviving cropper population. This would represent all those who were born during the hundred years preceding the demise of the sharecropping system, but were not alive during the last year of the system.

At the beginning of the sharecropping period in 1865, there existed approximately five million live black croppers. This number represented the surviving residues of slightly in excess of nine million live black births. By 1965, approximately twenty-two million black survivors stood at the threshold of a new social status as "free wage laborers." These survivors were the residues of some forty-five million live births over the preceding one hundred years. On net, therefore, some eighteen million live black issues out of the wombs of sharecropping mothers during the previous hundred years succumbed to death from unrecompensed labor.

An average of some 180,000 annual deaths among the members of the families of black sharecroppers provided the sacrificial lambs in the accumulation of material wealth in the society at large. How much this means in monetary terms must be staggering. Assuming an average life span of fifty years would yield the equivalent production of material goods involving nine million man years of labor per year. We would assume that the lion's share of the accumulated wealth found its way into the stock of capital and stimulated a most rapid and sustained growth in industry and commerce outside of the south from the end of the Civil War to the middle 1960s.

The major role of the political state was to enforce the rules of creation and acquisition of landlord private property. In time, the laws and customs known as "Jim Crow" became the bane of the black sharecroppers. Segregated institutions, providing separate accommodations and services to the blacks sprang up everywhere. Physical threats and actual infliction of violence upon the flesh attended the croppers' families. Elementary laws of capitalist private property which were etched in the organic law of the national political state in the thirteenth, fourteenth, and fifteenth amendments to the constitution were denied effective application to the black cropper. Everywhere, the local political state and its complementary private institutions conspired to keep the cropper in his exploited place. In the meantime, the national capitalist political state looked away in conspiracy of accommodation to the rulers of the southern sharecropping enclave.

The basic contradiction of the system inhered in the black struggle for survival. This was manifested in the continuing and relentless exertion of excruciatingly hard External Labor in the production of cotton and other material goods. Such External Labor was phased in synchronous alternation with the correspondingly difficult exertion of Internal Labor in the production of the sharecropping population. In direct opposition to these exertions of labor were the equal, but opposing, forces of the sharecropping contractual relations, enforced by the landlords and merchants in conjunction with the iron fist of the political state and its coteries of complementary private institutions.

The shackles of the sharecropping system would soon bend out of kilter from an imbalance of these two opposing forces. The system would soon be rent asunder and destroyed by a black revolution of historic moment.

The great black migration as social revolution

The sharecropping system was installed shortly after the Civil War partly at the bidding of the black freedmen. A rudimentary system of agricultural wage payments was attempted in which the planters tried to reinstitute the plantation gang labor methods not unlike those which prevailed under slavery. Mistrust and dissatisfaction drove the former slaves towards a sharecropping arrangement. Especially when such arrangements would stipulate fifty-fifty sharing, the freedmen were encouraged to think that they would not be cheated. After all, it didn't require any calculating ability to understand "one for you, one for me," until the total product became exhausted.

Once in place, however, there were many and devious ways in which the cropper could be cheated out of his contractual share. In any case, the accumulation of wealth in this society was such as to reproduce the feudal relations over and over again.

Among other things, the cropper was reproduced as a cropper, accumulating no material goods. This result was a consequence of the fact that the cropper's share of the product of his labor could be converted only into the barest minimum quantity of food necessary for his family's reproduction.

Under slavery the *per capita* income distribution among the

Black sharecropping and capitalism in the US

slaves was perfectly equal, and averaged zero. Under the sharecropping system, per capita income distribution among the population of croppers was also approximately equal, but with an average value equal to the cost of a minimum bundle of food required for reproduction of the individual.

The struggle for survival became very difficult. Some tried to resolve the problem by acquiring land ownership. By the first decade of the twentieth century such ownership had reached a peak at some fifteen million acres. But most of the plots were relatively small subsistence farms, incapable of being exploited as commercial ventures. For the next six decades black land ownership declined, until by 1965 it was estimated at less than six million acres.

Meantime, the peak in land ownership coincided with another phenomenon that was to revolutionize the system. A mass of black live bodies entered a social stream, and then a social river, and then a social inundation of the flood plains of the river, flowing down to the cities of the nation. Blacks had been migrating before. During the slave period they were sold or otherwise shipped off to the burgeoning cotton lands. They slashed and burned and cleared millions of acres of virgin lands, from the eastern shores of Maryland, Virginia, the Carolinas, to Tennessee, Alabama, Mississippi, Arkansas, Louisiana, Texas.

With the end of slavery they exercised their newly won freedom by migrating voluntarily to the cities of the south. By the turn of the century this process was quite pronounced. During World War I, however, the pace of movement stepped up, with a noticeable branch of the migrant stream moving from south to north. When this movement came to an end by the middle of the 1960s, literally the entire population of blacks had been emptied off the land and had become the most urbanized of an urban America. Moreover, almost half of these people now resided outside of the south, the cradle of their American beginnings and the exclusive domain of their development.

The migration was a young people's movement. They left voluntarily; but a series of economic circumstances aided the process. Fundamentally, they were forcibly ejected by capital – the very same capital that was formed out of their unpaid labor upon the land. This expropriation of the blacks from the cotton fields was a classic case of a landless peasant in the process of transformation into a wage laborer. The direct commercialization of cotton agriculture had begun in earnest. The profits made by the financial and textile interests of the north out of sharecropper unpaid labor were beginning to flow back to the south, this time in the form of tractors, cotton gins, pickers, and other implements.

Here was historic irony. The cropper was being ejected from the land and thereby from his economic class status by the very selfsame labor he exerted for survival, but which at the same time was stolen from him to enrich the pockets of others. Indeed, his "liberated" status was wrought by his own endeavors, even though controlled and directed by others for their own private gain.

The process of displacement of the cropper by capital and the transformation of sharecropping property relations into capitalist private property relations could not take place without the conscious acquiescence of the cropper. In fact, in the beginning, at the second decade of the twentieth century, it was the cropper who took the initial and decisive step. Young blacks, later followed by parents and relatives, wrenched themselves away from the cropper system and voluntarily journeyed northward to join the general American wage working class.

This act was not an easy one to pursue; nor was it without violent opposition from the rulers of the roost. Active recruiters of black people for work in the north were arrested on vague charges, made to pay exorbitant license fees, and generally harassed in numerous ways. But it was the cropper who bore the brunt of vengeance of the political state, its formal and informal police arms, and the private institutions. More stringent "Jim Crow" laws came on the books; klan violence, including murder, stepped up in frequency and impact. This was no time for reverie on the part of the cropper. He had to devise ways to evade the system in the active quest for freedom. Stealing away in the night, making up stories of sick and dying relatives in the north, hiding out in the woods by day – these were a few of the devices resorted to.

As the tidal waves of migration swelled, the rivers flowed down to the north, carrying a people in collective revolutionary transition. Very few of the black migrants consciously understood the nature of the revolution. And those who had already ended the sojourn lamented the steady coming of the new arrivals.

Nevertheless, they flowed across the east coast, from the southern tip of Florida, through Miami, Jacksonville, Charleston,

Raleigh, Norfolk, Richmond, Baltimore, District of Columbia, Wilmington, Philadelphia, Camden, Newark, New York, New Haven, Hartford, Providence, Boston.

They flooded another river astride the banks of the great Mississippi river, as if in defiance of the southern currents which took that mighty waterway southward to the Gulf of Mexico. By car and truck and bus and by the "fast train" of the Illinois Central Railroad they moved relentlessly on from New Orleans through Baton Rouge, Natchez, Vicksburg, Jackson, Memphis, St. Louis, Chicago. Some then branched off to Gary and Detroit. Still others wended their way to Milwaukee and Minneapolis-St. Paul.

Lastly, the migrant stream moved in a third river bed, going north by west from Arkansas, Louisiana, Texas, Kansas, Oklahoma to Colorado, Arizona, California, Washington.

When the process was complete – sometime during the latter half of the 1960s – former black sharecroppers had enriched the music and art and literature and recreation of America. Some ignorant Americans got a first exposure to the brilliant, but not new, contributions of a group of young black intelligentsia; they called their impressions a renaissance; they also said it got started in Harlem. Others became aware of the works of some black purveyors of a music called blues and jazz; they even distinguished a few varieties and labelled them New Orleans and Memphis and St. Louis and Chicago. Little did they know that they were tracing the footsteps of a revolution. Still others discovered that these black people were natural thespians and made them act the buffoon in the entertainment medium called the movies.

The revolutionary transformation came to visible moments in the so-called Civil Rights movement of the 1960s. A preacher was to give it the verbal articulation and personal confrontational leadership it desperately needed to stir the conscience of the nation. A few other young men and women tried to enunciate their visions of a more potent revolutionary route to the ultimate solution; they became the new household prophets of another tomorrow, not now.

Meantime, the civil rights movement carried out its assault against the vestiges of the system of black sharecropping labor exploitation. It focussed its efforts on the remaining legal and social institutional framework – politics, education, religion, public accommodation, local legislation, local courts, local police, vigilantism, federal statutes, federal constitutional guarantees.

Some of the articulate prophets were assassinated. Others were thrown into prisons in an unconscionable manner. But the people nevertheless prevailed.

Thus, the civil rights movement was the capstone of the revolution which had commenced fifty years earlier. It marked the end of the sharecropping system of black labor exploitation for good. It established for the first time the legal basis for the existence of a class of black wage laborers by imbedding into the constitution and in statutory acts and administrative practices the concept of private proprietorship of the black laborer in his ability to work. Thereby was cemented his right to sell that ability to the highest bidder on the open market for a money wage, and not for a direct share in kind of the product of his labor.

By the end of the 1960s black Americans entered upon a new phase in their social transformation. For the first time, as a people, they had become a *bona fide* class of free wage laborers. This meant, however, that they were now separated from the land and from their food supply. Wage dependence or employment by white capitalist employers or white capitalist government agencies, would now be their lot.

(Black Americans now represent the last great reproducible segment of the general American wage working class. But they enter upon this phase of their existence with a difference. They are stamped with black skins by the unique historical experiences of economic oppression in America.) How they interrelate with their fellow white wage laborers and how they impact white capitalists are the big economic agendas facing them.

7 The black wage labor system and the rate of capital accumulation in the United States, 1965–

The black wage laboring system is an integral and inseparable part of the national capitalist economy of the United States. We deal with it here as a subsystem only for analytical purposes. A justification for this procedure is that at least for the forseeable future black people will continue to be reproduced as black people, to the almost total exclusion of other people in the nation.

Another justification for dealing with the black wage laboring subsystem is to sharpen our understanding of the special and differential effects of direct capitalist exploitation on the present condition of pauperism among black people.

The black wage laboring system is framed by a series of interactions among black people themselves as well as between black people and non-black peoples within the United States. Within the black population, black wage laborers interact with black capitalists. However, this latter class of black people is so negligible that we generally ignore it in our analysis. For all practical purposes, then, the black population may be considered to be a homogeneous class of wage laborers.

The most fundamental interaction within this labor system is the act of reproduction of the black population as a black wage laboring population. This is an organic social embrace which unites members of the black population with each other to produce the human basis of their continuing existence as a black population. It also involves the interlocking entanglements of black people with non-black people to produce the material means of their survival. It also involves a host of other supporting relationships which are absolutely necessary to make the black reproduction process a stable and continuous historical venture.

Within the black population, the Internal Labor Process provides for individual families to produce their offspring, to maintain the living status of their existing members, and to possibly add to their numbers over time. This process supersedes the former sharecropping Internal Labor era.

Blacks interact in a very important way with the class of non-black capitalists to exert External Labor in the production of the potential material means of their survival. Since they are employed (although in some cases rather sparsely) in every industry, they effectively interact with all members of the class of non-black capitalists in the nation.

In the act of External Labor black workers co-operate with each other as well as with the class of non-black wage laborers, under the control and direction of the class of non-black capitalists. In the detailed division of labor within the workplace each black and non-black worker carries out assigned tasks in the act of producing commodities for the private ownership of members of the non-black capitalist class. In the social division of External Labor connecting the various industries, blacks across the land co-operate with non-black wage workers in the production of the material social product.

Another very important interaction also takes place between members of the black population and members of the non-black wage laboring class. The two groups are in active conflict for employment in limited numbers of jobs. The textbooks characterize this conflict as "competition;" but the hard reality is that under the conditions that blacks entered the wage laboring system, the struggle to survive on the basis of having legitimate access to money wages has taken on the characteristics of warfare among all the wage seekers.

We must also call attention to the almost complete absence of Internal Labor interactions between members of the black population and members of the non-black wage working class. While the possibility exists, it has nevertheless been of minimal significance to the present day.

Wealth in the black wage laboring system is owned and privately accumulated in the form of capital by members of the class of non-black capitalists. It arises out of the effective ability of this class to bind black workers to their material means of survival, in both a commodity producing and commodity consuming mode. Thus, the material wealth which results from this bond is the legitimate private property of the capitalists upon whom black wage workers must depend for money wages, and from whom they must purchase their material means of survival with those very same money wages.

The economic classes

The entire class of wage laborers in 1982 consisted of approximately two-thirds to nine-tenths of the population of the United States of some 235 million. The black wage laboring class, in turn, comprises about 11.6 per cent of the total wage working class.

The black wage laborer originated out of the demise of the sharecropping system which prevailed in the cotton south for a hundred years following on the Civil War. The first *bona fide* appearance of this class came in the initial migrations of a few newly freed slaves to the cities of the south. It was, however, the Great Migration, commencing during the second decade of the twentieth century, which set in motion the necessary conditions for the formation of this class.

Members of the wage earning class are distributed among social units called households. There are approximately ten million such black households, with some 25 per cent consisting of single individuals. The remaining 75 per cent are generally called family units.

Fifty-five per cent of the black family units consist of husband, wife, and children; 5 per cent consist of male adults and children; the remaining 40 per cent consist of female adults and children. There is a rapidly growing trend towards this latter type of family; for example, more than 50 per cent of the babies born alive to black mothers now come into these families.

Black households vary in membership size from one to twenty, characterized by a highly right-skewed distribution. Eighty per cent of these households contain from one to four members; the average membership is three and a half.

The ages of individuals within black households vary from less than one year of age to over one hundred years of age. About one-third are under fifteen years; less than 10 per cent are over sixty-four; about 60 per cent range between fifteen and sixty-four. In general, this population is relatively young.

Females exceed males in numbers within the black population, making up about fifty-three per cent. At the ages between birth and fourteen years, the number of black males slightly exceeds the number of black females. However, there is a steady decline from the lower through the higher age groups, such that by ages sixty-five and over, black males are only 40 per cent of the black population.

The black population did not have the opportunity to spin off a class of capitalists. Under slavery this was an impossibility; under sharecropping it was practically out of the question. Only in recent years have the opportunities arisen for the formation of a class of black capitalists. We estimate no more than fifteen thousand such individuals, inclusive of all family members.

The class of non-black capitalists had its rudimentary beginnings during the colonial period. Starting from small traders and merchants, they soon swelled their ranks with the New England slave traders, rum runners, exporters of agricultural products (tobacco, rice, indigo, timber), importers of foreign manufactured goods.

In time they became owners of the shipbuilding yards, railroads, iron foundries, steel mills, textile factories. With the expansion of the domestic market they multiplied. The war of national liberation from Great Britain provided tremendous opportunities for the amassing of huge fortunes from looting of British shipping and from sales to the armed forces.

By the end of the Civil War they had become the most powerful single economic force in the country. American economic life would thenceforth be directed by this class from the vantage point of a burgeoning array of commercial, financial, manufacturing, and service firms.

The operational instrument for a capitalist is the business firm. Each such firm must have on hand a given quantity of capital, distributed among equipment, raw materials, consumer goods, inventory of the specific commodity which the firm produces, and money. The firm may be owned individually, or under some joint arrangement.

The specific configuration of the capital stock is at one and the same time an indication of the technique of production as well as the type of capital which the firm produces. The technology dictates the detailed division of labor within the firm; that is to say, each of the different tasks which must be performed, the numbers of laborers who are to perform each task, and the overall co-ordinating plan of co-operation among the various laborers are all embodied in the capital owned by the firm.

On average, all firms which produce the same type of capital use the same technology. Differences in the quantities of capital owned by these firms are compounded of a common constant multiple of the elements which go to make the total capital stock. Of course, differences among capitalists in individual will, knowledge, temperament, assessment of business profitability, etc. will make for some random variations from the standard average configuration of capital.

In the United States today there are some fifteen million business firms. Together with hundreds of thousands of government agencies at all levels, these firms produce capital commodities of all types to the official estimated tune of over three trillion dollars.

Single proprietorships and partnerships dominate in numbers, with some twelve and one-half million firms. Corporations, on the other hand, represent less than two million firms, but they are privy to the lion's share of perhaps 90 per cent of all business receipts. Furthermore, there is a tremendous concentration of capital in just a few thousand of the largest corporations.

The types of capital which these firms produce may be classified in many ways. One such classification is "consumer goods, money, and material means of External Labor."

Another classification attempts to locate the capital in its position within an interconnected serial mode of production. "Primary" commodities refer to the direct products of human External Labor upon the soil. Agriculture, forestry, fishery, quarry, mine, ocean are the arenas for producing these commodities.

A most important member of the primary group is "raw food." The metal ores, particularly any one out of which money is fashioned, are also important members of this group. In general, primary commodities have the characteristic of being the material substrata of all types of capital.

A second classification identifies "intermediary" commodities. These include commodities produced by manufacture, construction, business service (transportation, communication, public utility, wholesale trade, finance, real estate, insurance, etc.). These commodities originate from the processing of primary commodities.

A third group is referred to as "final" commodities. This group consists of "consumer goods" which are primarily destined to be used by laborers in the Internal Labor Process. They result from the retail trade and personal service activities.

In sum, the black wage laboring system is a capitalist political economy deeply and integrally imbedded in the capitalist political economy of the United States. It is a relatively new era, commencing about the middle of the 1960s, although it was in the making for some fifty years before that.

It involves the social reproduction of the black population under the special historical and institutional mechanisms of capitalism. One important aspect of the peculiar nature of this system is that practically the entire black population forms a homogeneous class of wage laborers. Hence, capital accumulation based on material wealth produced by black workers is the private property of non-black capitalists within the nation.

The market for black human energy

The market for black human energy is the institutional process which acts as a conduit for distributing black human energy in the form of commodities, from the black Internal Labor Process where it is produced, to the black External Labor Process where it is used. Simultaneously, and as a necessary adjunct to the movement of human energy, this market provides a conduit for distributing money wages from capitalist owners of the External Labor Process to black wage laborer owners of the Internal Labor Process.

The essential functions of this market is a determination of the total number of black workers who will get employment in a particular firm and the total wages which will be paid to these employed workers by the owners of that firm. Aggregating over all firms and all black workers yields a specific distribution of black employment among the various firms, and a specific distribution of wages among the various black households. These are the final outcomes of this market apparatus.

The operations of this market are circumscribed in the real world by the existence of a relatively large number of unemployed black wage laborers. This means that there is intense competition, if not conflict, among members of the black population for a limited number of employment opportunities from capitalists.

Young black workers are least successful in this market compared with prime age black workers. Female black workers fare worse than their black male counterparts. Elderly black workers are at greater risk than prime age black workers. Black high school and elementary school dropouts find it much more difficult to get employment than black high school and college graduates. Unmarried black mothers with young children at home are at much greater risk than black married mothers with no children at home.

Black workers are also in intense competitive warfare with their non-black wage laboring counterparts. As relative newcomers to the wage laboring class they are at extreme disadvantage in the overall attempt to secure employment. At best, they seem to be most successful in moving into employment slots deemed undesirable by the non-black wage laboring class.

On the demand side the determinants of employment are functions of the amount of money a capitalist brings to market to purchase specific quantities and types of human energy consistent with the capital configuration owned by the firm.

Given this demand for human energy, the maximum wage bill the capitalist is willing to pay to the prospective group of employed laborers is determined by arbitrarily setting a target rate of profit for the firm's operations. The target is, of course, based on knowledge of actual profitability experience of the industry, knowledge of conditions in the economy at large, and other personal peculiarities and whims of the individual capitalist himself.

Given the wage bill and the number of workers (carriers of human energy) to be employed, the demand wage can be calculated. This is the maximum wage which the capitalist could conceivably pay equally to every worker without overspending the total wage bill. However, there is no compelling reason in theory or in practice why the capitalist should be an egalitarian wage payer. The profit target being assured, the specific distribution of wages among the various workers is determined by considerations outside the market place.

It is a well documented fact that practically every capitalist firm opts for a right-skewed wage distribution. An important outgrowth of such a distribution is that it is capable of forming the basis for a pyramidal hierarchy of control over the work force. Every capitalist must manage his External Labor Process. That is to say, he must have specific ways of exercising control over the will of his workers if the process is to function at all. The wage distribution thus provides one possible instrumentality for this purpose. It is indeed a management tool.

Once a hierarchical wage distribution is established, then all sorts of rationalizations may be put forward by the capitalist to justify its unequal impact. The level of formal schooling, experience on the job, maturity, intelligence, aptitude, attitude, etc. are some of the so-called "qualifications" which rationalize the unequal wages paid for different tasks within the detailed division of labor in the workplace. But we know full well that gender, youth, kinship distance are potent discretionary factors underlying the unequal distribution of wage payments. And most important of all for our analysis is that black wage laborers receive less than favorite treatment in this regard.

We want to stress once more the degrees of freedom available to the capitalist to choose among different distributions of wages. The particular one chosen is based on considerations having to do with the onerous task of bending the will of the workers to conform to that of the owners of the firm in the production of the commodities in accordance with the preconceived plan of such owners. Whatever distribution "best" aids and abets in this task is the one which will be chosen.

Each capitalist differs from any other with respect to the type of firm owned, the quantity of capital owned, the personal ability to implement the technology implicit in the capital owned, the rate of profit targeted, and a host of other attributes. We would therefore expect to find a wide distribution of the demand wage rate among the millions of business firms. Such a distribution, however, would exhibit many of the characteristics of the wage distribution within a single firm. We must, however, keep the distinction in mind between the distribution of wages among workers within a single firm and the distribution of the demand wage rate among all firms.

On the supply side, the number of household members as well as the age distribution of the members and other characteristics dictate the technology of production of human energy. More particularly, the quantity and types of consumer goods – food, clothing, housing, etc. – required to produce human energy are determined by the configuration of household membership itself.

These requirements, in turn, dictate the quantity of Internal Labor which must be generated, and hence the quantity and value of human energy to be produced by that labor.

The worker's household members determine the consumer goods bill by setting a maximum rate of exploitation which it is willing to endure in order to keep its membership alive. Such a targeted rate may be based on past experience, knowledge of other similar workers' household circumstances, and personal assessments of the future economic prospects. In any case, the exploitation target, set as a percentage of the projected value of the human energy to be produced, yields an estimate of the consumer goods bill. Thus, the minimum supply wage income at which the household in question will sell a given quantity of human energy is determinate.

A given worker's household differs from any other worker's household with respect to the number of members, the age distribution of the members, knowledge of implementation of the technology of Internal Labor, understanding of the prospects in the economy at large, etc. We would therefore expect that the supply wage rate will be extremely widely distributed among all the workers' households.

A most important empirical fact about this market must be noted. Black employment, at least since 1960, has maintained a proportion of the total employment in the nation almost exactly consistent with the black proportion of the total national US surviving population. In 1960, for example, black proportion of civilian employment was 10.5 per cent; in 1979 it was 11.1 per cent. The corresponding surviving black population proportions were 11.5 per cent in both years. These numbers may be coincidentally related; however, it is also possible that there is an essential connection between survival and employment. After all, employment is, in a sense, a necessary condition for access to food and other consumables.

The market for black human energy as we have thus far depicted it leaves black workers in a rather special position. Prior to 1970, during the transition period towards becoming wage laborers, black ex-sharecroppers had to take whatever employment they could get. They came from a political economy in which the survival kit which they received in recompense for their External Labors consisted of the barest minimum food requirements and not much more.

In the new wage system these people could therefore reproduce themselves at rather low levels of material intake. The point is that any employment, at practically any wage level, could be paid to this group which was entering the wage system under conditions in which they were not yet socialized to the capitalist system of political economy. They thus were passive takers of whatever the market offered. Any offer secured their escape from the former historical era from which they were fleeing. The demand side dominated the market.

Today, however, the black worker has sufficiently long experience in the wage labor system. We would guess that during the 1980s black employment proportions and the corresponding average black wage rate should show significant improvement over the 1970s.

A summary of some of the salient features of the market for black human energy must include the facts that actual wages paid to black workers are widely distributed within any given firm; and that actual wages received by black households throughout the nation are also widely distributed. Unequal distribution of wages among black households is therefore an endemic condition within the market for black human energy. It is important to note in passing that among these unequal wages are a significant number of zero wages, corresponding to the unemployed. It is also important to remember that the distribution of black household wages is highly right-skewed; that is to say, the vast majority of such wage payments are concentrated among the lowest segments of the distribution.

Because blacks came on the historical tail end of the national capitalist system as wage laborers, they find themselves at great disadvantage in this market compared to their non-black counterparts. They are generally confined to jobs which pay the least. In the national distribution of wages, therefore, black households form a greater density at the lowest levels of wage than their non-black counterparts.

In 1969 less than seven million blacks were effective operators within the market for black human energy. These are the ones who were actually employed by capitalist firms and government agencies throughout all industries in the nation.

Classifying all firms into fifty-two industry groups gave us a ranking of these groups as "excellent," "good," or "poor" employers of black laborers.

Eighteen poor employing industry groups gave black laborers between 3 and 8 per cent of their jobs; seventeen good employing industry groups gave black laborers between 8 and 10 per cent of their jobs; and seventeen excellent employment industry groups gave blacks between 10 and 31 per cent of their jobs.

In the poor category, ranked in decreasing incidence of "poorness," were mining, miscellaneous machinery manufacture, insurance, aircraft manufacture, publishing, miscellaneous durable goods manufacture, wholesale trade, fabricated metals manufacture, miscellaneous finance/real estate, miscellaneous repair service, business service, communication, ordnance manufacture, chemical products manufacture, railway, and paper products manufacture.

In the good category, ranked in increasing order of "goodness," were primary non-ferrous metal manufacture, rubber/plastics manufacture, entertainment/recreation, miscellaneous professional service, auto dealer/gas station, general merchandise retail store, trucking/warehousing, construction, stone/glass/clay products manufacture, auto repair service, agriculture/forestry/fishery, retail clothing store, utilities/sanitary services, public education, miscellaneous transportation equipment manufacture.

In the excellent category, ranked in ascending order of "excellence," were welfare/religious/non-profit organizations, food products manufacture, miscellaneous retail store, miscellaneous transportation services, apparel product manufacture, public administration, textile mill product manufacture, miscellaneous non-durable product manufacture, furniture/fixture manufacture, motor vehicle manufacture, primary ferrous metal manufacture, miscellaneous health services, hotel/lodging places, hospitals, lumber/wood product manufacture, eating/drinking places, personal services other than hotel.

The poor employing industries hired 1.4 million black laborers, or 20.4 per cent of total black employment. The good employing industries hired 2.0 million black laborers, or 28.6 per cent of the total. The best industries employed 3.5 million black laborers, or 51.0 per cent of the total.

Another way of classifying the types of industries which employ black laborers is to consider them as producers of primary, intermediary, or final commodities as we have defined them earlier.

Primary industries employed slightly less than 300,000 black laborers, or 4.1 per cent of the total. Intermediary industries employed four million black laborers, or 57.7 per cent of the total. Final industries employed 2.7 million black workers, or 38.2 per cent of the total.

During 1969 we estimate that the distribution of wage payments among all black households aggregated to a total of approximately $40 billions. Our estimate is that during 1981 some eleven million black households were receiving wage incomes approximating $140 billions. We would also project that the distribution of black employment among the various industries should substantially change for the better compared to 1969.

Thus far, we have not described the impacts of trade union organization among black workers, organizations of business firms, and government intervention in this market. We do not attempt to play down the important roles and influences of these institutions on the outcomes in this market. We will have to come back to them in the sequel.

Money wages serve the function of purchasing the material means of survival of the black population. Purchase of such materials, however, takes place under another distinct set of social relations in the market for black consumer goods.

The market for black consumer goods

The market for black consumer goods is the institutional process which provides a conduit for the distribution of consumer goods to black households. It is the effective mechanism for transferring consumer goods from the capitalist-owned External Labor Process where they are created to the Internal Labor Process where they are used by members of the black population.

Simultaneously with the distribution of consumer goods, there goes hand in hand a distribution, in the opposite direction, of money in the form of prices paid for the consumer goods. Black households are made to yield up to non-black capitalists certain sums of money in exchange for the consumer goods received.

All the interactions between workers and capitalists in this market can be summarized in two distributions – the distribution of consumer goods among black households for their personal use, and the corresponding distribution of money prices (expenditures) for these goods among the various non-black capitalists. Aggregating these distributions over all black households and all capitalists gives the total consumer expenditures made by all black households to all capitalists and the total quantity of consumer goods sold by all capitalists to all black households.

On the demand side of this market are the employed black workers who play the role of buyers of consumer goods. The determinants of the quantities of the various goods bought by each black household are dictated by the technology of Internal Labor implicit in the quantity and characteristics of the black household membership. The expenditures for such quantity depend upon the amount of money available to the household.

However the contents of the bundles of consumer goods purchased by different black households may vary, each household is bound to purchase a quantity of food sufficient to create the energies which maintain the lives of its existing members. Food is the primal consumer commodity. It takes first and unchallenged claim against the money available to each black household. Therefore, among black households the required quantity of food purchased varies directly with black household membership, regardless of the differences in money available to these households. Hence, the distribution of the quantity of food purchased by black households mirrors and reflects the distribution of black family membership.

Purchase of non-food consumer goods is limited by the residual monies available to the black household after food requirements have been purchased.

Let us assume that there exists an unambiguously defined physical quantity of foods which constitutes the standard average *per capita* requirement for the generation of Internal Labor. Let us further measure the quantity of money available to a given black household as the maximum number of standard *per capita* food units which that money can purchase.

Under these assumptions, money available minus size of household membership defines quantity of non-food purchases. Among black households with the same quantity of money available, therefore, the quantity of non-food purchases must vary inversely with the size of the black household.

Finally, among black households of the same size, the quantity of non-food purchases varies directly with the quantity of money available to the household.

It follows from these considerations that the quantity of food and non-food consumer goods purchased will be widely distributed among black households, depending on the distributions of number of household members and available money. More particularly, household size (and related physical and social characteristics of the members) is the most dominant factor. It dictates household food requirements. Non-food purchases take up the residual money available.

The market mechanism operates in such a way that no buyer may come to the relationship without possessing a given sum of money with which to make purchases. Thus, black households are assumed to do just that. But what is the source of this money? We shall have to come back to this in the sequel.

On the supply side capitalists who sell consumer goods are the other party to this market relationship. They come to market with a stock of consumer goods which results from the previous operations of the External Labor Process. We assume that the supply prices at which they offer these goods conform to their profit-targeting conditions in their control and direction of the External Labor Process.

The interactions between black buyers and capitalist sellers bring about a mutuality of quantities bought and money paid for these quantities.

It must be noted that black buyers do not relate directly to all capitalists in this market. The range of interactions is limited to all black workers on the one hand and only those capitalists whose firms produce consumer goods on the other hand. Black workers employed by capitalist firms that produce primary and intermediary commodities cannot spend their wages directly with the firms that employ them. What this means is that in the aggregate, the total sales made by consumer goods producing capitalist firms cannot exceed (a) the black wage bill of primary commodity producing firms, plus (b) the black wage bill of intermediary commodity producing capitalist firms, (c) plus the black wage bill of consumer producing capitalist firms. These three sums exhaust the total wage incomes of all black households.

We need to specify the various quantities of consumer goods which black households purchase from capitalist firms in the real world. If we assume that the *per capita* food requirements of blacks are the same as those within the general US population, then we can state that in 1981 the black population purchased an aggregate of close to twenty million metric tons of food.

Fifty-six per cent of the total quantity of food was in the form of plant products; 44 per cent consisted of animal products. Among the animal products, cattle was the source of the major share, comprising close to 75 per cent. Poultry provided 14 per cent, pigs provided 10 per cent, sheep and fish provided the remainder.

The plant products were mainly grain, vegetable, fruit, potato, refined sugar, fat, coffee, and tea in declining order of importance.

A more refined estimate of specific purchases by black households should take account of the larger concentration of black wage incomes in the lowest end of the national distribution of wages. The total tonnage of food purchase may not be a bad estimate; but the distribution among the various elements would certainly diverge from the national pattern.

For example, we would expect that in the animal products group, black households would give greatest weight to poultry, pig, and fish instead of cattle. Grain, fat, potato would likewise play a major role, as compared to the national pattern among the plant products.

The non-food items in the black household budget are purchased out of residual income after food is accounted for. The larger households would have the most difficulty reserving any such residual income. And, naturally, the lower the wage income, the more unlikely that much of a residual would be available at all.

We may therefore tentatively conclude that black wage incomes have not yet been sufficiently large to allow but the most meager access to non-food consumer goods. Dilapidated housing, poor health care, very little private transportation, relatively little higher education seem to be the rule. In addition, we also know that there is still great room for improvement in the diet in terms of more nutritionally adequate items.

We have now invoked the source of money used to purchase black consumer commodities as money wage incomes. It should now be obvious that these two black markets operate as a unity within the capitalist political economy. We should therefore explore the nature of this unity.

The unity of the two black markets

The market for black human energy is the legitimate institutional mechanism by which non-black capitalists are able to get private ownership of black human energy. This same market is also the legitimate institutional mechanism by which black laborers are able to acquire private ownership of money. Buying and selling thus dialectically abrogate the private property rights of commodity owners, while at the very instant reinstitute private property rights. For the black laborer, private ownership of human energy disappears; long live private property rights in money wage! For the capitalist, private property rights in money wages disappear; long live private property rights in black human energy!

The market for black consumer goods is the legitimate institutional mechanism by which black wage laborers acquire private ownership of consumer goods. This same market is likewise the institutional mechanism by which the capitalists acquire private ownership of money. Like the other market a dialectical process of abrogating private property rights while simultaneously reinstituting private property rights is in operation. For the black worker, private property rights in money disappear; long live private property rights in consumer goods! For the capitalist, private property rights in consumer goods disappear; long live private property rights in money!

As a unity, however, the two markets together typify the act of converting one type of commodity into its opposite. Looked at from the perspective of the black laborer, human energy is converted into consumer goods. From the vantage point of the capitalist, consumer goods have been converted into black human energy. Finally, the two opposite, but complementary, conversions are made possible by the conversion of capitalist privately owned money wages into capitalist privately owned money prices.

On yet another fundamental level, the synthetic bond typified by the unity of the two markets puts the black laborer at the disposal of the non-black capitalist; simultaneously, it puts consumer goods at the disposal of the black laborer. All the time, however, the bonding is of a specific market nature. These two markets thus establish the legitimate preconditions under which black laborers will be able to exercise their human energies in the creation of their material means of survival; at the same time the markets also establish the legitimate quantity of the material means of survival which will be returned to the black worker.

The conversion of privately owned capitalist money wages into privately owned capitalist money prices has significant implications for the overall political economy. In the aggregate, this means that the sum total of money wages paid out by capitalists to all black employed laborers returns to them in the sum total of prices or expenditures paid by black wage laborers to capitalists. Money thus acts as a catalyst, facilitating the black laborers' conversion of their human energies into consumer goods, but coming out of the exchanges in the same form and the same quantity as it entered. This is the epitome of money in its traditional role of medium of exchange.

The meaning of all this is quite clear. A black worker sells his human energy to a non-black capitalist for a sum of money wages. In turn, he spends the money to buy the consumer goods required by members of his household. The expenditure of the money, however, is generally not made directly to the specific capitalist to which his human energy was sold. As a matter of fact, there is a greater than 60 per cent chance that a given black worker will not spend his wage income directly with the firm that employs him.

There is a dynamic in operation in which the two markets together establish a relationship between each capitalist firm and the black workers whom it employs in order to ensure that the wages paid to such workers reflux back into the coffers of the firm. One way in which this can actually take place is that a specific type of relationship must be established between primary and intermediary commodity-producing firms on the one hand, and consumer-goods-producing firms on the other hand. The latter firms must serve as conduits for returning the wages paid by the former firms back into their cash registers. But this sort of relationship takes place outside of market activity.

The private disposition which capitalists will make of the black human energy is to use such energy in the External Labor Process to produce material commodities. This is accomplished by putting the black laborers who are carriers of this energy to perform labor. But this activity is outside the market spheres.

The private disposition which black laborers will make of the consumer goods is to use such goods in the Internal Labor Process to produce black human energy. This is accomplished by consuming these goods upon their persons. But this activity is outside of the market spheres.

The joint operation of the two markets is thus the paragon of the binding force of capitalist private property – a material synthesis of the black wage laborers and their material means of survival. The specific form of the synthesis is the commodity form. At this stage of our analysis, however, its fundamental meaning is that it is this peculiar institutional arrangement which determines the legitimate terms on which black labor is exploited.

But the bonding of black laborers and their means of survival is at the same time the legitimate institutional link-up of the two phases of black labor. Black External Labor is enabled to operate in handshaking synchrony with Black Internal Labor through the mediating role of the joint operation of the two black markets.

The black External Labor Process

The black External Labor Process is the set of institutional activities carried on in business firms and government agencies in which black wage laborers, under the direction of their capitalist employers, produce commodities in the form of capital.

Each firm is distinguished by ownership of a specific quantitative configuration of the various types of capital. The capital configuration embodies the technology of External Labor, the plan of production of capital. It sets the operating parameters for a given firm and its relationship to all other firms in the society.

The intermediary commodities which form part of the capital stock of the given firm, and which will be used up in current production, were purchased from a specific set of firms and must be replaced by this same set of firms at the end of the production period in order to keep the capital stock from deteriorating. These relationships constitute the so-called backward linkages in production.

The backward linkages exemplify the social division of labor in the production of a given firm's commodity. On a national level, these interactions can boggle the mind. Automobile production, for example, is said to require the use of more than ten thousand distinct intermediary products. All of these must be already owned by the automobile firm as part of its capital stock in the requisite quantities before one automobile can come off the assembly line. In short, the production of a particular firm's product requires a tight cooperative linkage with a large number of specialized firms, related together in a serially coordinated manner.

The capital configuration also determines the detailed division of labor within the firm. Each specific task to be performed, the number and types of human energy required for each task, the quantity of intermediary commodities which will accommodate each task, the nature of the coordinating efforts, the methods of control of the work force, the quantity of capital which is to be produced within a given period of time – these are but a small sample of the technological impact of the capital configuration on management of the employed black wage laborers.

The capital configuration also dictates the type of product to be produced. The type of product, in turn, determines the interactions between any given firm and all other firms and all other wage workers who are potential users of the firm's products.

If the given firm produces consumer goods, then its sales must be directed towards workers. If, on the other hand, it produces intermediary commodities, then its sales efforts are generally directed towards other business firms. In the former case, it must sell a minimum sufficient to recover its own wage payments, in addition to the value of the intermediary commodities it used up in current production. In the latter case, it must sell to firms which produce consumer goods a quantity of product at least equal in value to the wages paid to its own workers.

The forward and backward linkages establish a set of production relations which not only join business firms together in a serially connected symbiotic network; but they also establish a direct web of cooperation among workers in a given firm and all other workers throughout the economy. It should be noted that a necessary condition for all of these interactions to take place in the External Labor Process is the joint operation of the two markets we have described heretofore.

Black External Labor can be succinctly described as a transformation of black human energy into capital, under the direction, control, and private ownership of capitalist owners of business firms. A necessary condition for this to take place is that the two markets must have operated previously, so that (a) the ownership of black human energy has already been legitimately acquired by the owners of capitalist firms; (b) the proportion of the prospective fruits of the External Labor of black laborers which such laborers can legitimately claim is fixed by the wage bargains; (c) the cooperative relationship between black workers in the given firm and all other workers is established by the overall distribution of black wages; and (d) the terms of conversion of the black workers' shares of the products into consumer goods are established by the prices paid by black workers for these commodities.

The quantity of External Labor generated by black workers during a given period of time is an essential characteristic of the commodities which that labor produces. Indeed, the material form of the commodities produced is so much congealed External Labor activity. Analytically, we may separate out two mutually exclusive parts of External Labor – paid labor, measured by the wage payments; and unpaid, measured by the excess of inputs of External Labor over the wage payments. This latter quantity is what the textbooks generally refer to as profits.

External Labor, however, is an activity which comes to an end. It results in the creation of capital and therefore it may alternatively be measured by its product. The value of the total product may be divided into that part which is sold to workers plus the remainder. That is to say, in value terms the total product is equal to workers' consumer expenditures plus the remainder of the product. This latter part is usually referred to as investments.

In the case of an individual firm, what we have referred to as profits is a gross figure which must be divided up among the firm and its suppliers of primary and intermediary commodities. Similarly, what we have referred to as investments is a gross figure for the individual firm and represents that part of the product which must be used to replace primary and intermediary commodities used up in current production.

In the case of the nation as a whole, however, the distinction between gross and net is of no consequence.

A summary description of the Black External Labor Process would specify empirically the (a) distribution of the quantity of External Labor generated by black workers among all firms; (b) distribution of quantity, type and value of capital produced by all black workers among the various firms; (c) distribution of profits among all firms on the basis of employing black workers. The aggregation of these distributions over the entire economy is of the utmost importance in understanding the real impact of this most fundamental activity.

Within the External Labor Process black laborers are made to perform certain specified tasks within the firms which employ them. During 1969, near the beginning of the black wage laboring period, very few tasks dominated the role of blacks. Maid and janitor in household, office, hospital; unspecialized laborer, including operative of all types; miscellaneous clerk; assembler; miscellaneous specialized laborer; practical nurse; social and recreational worker – these constituted the most potent tasks within the division of labor performed by black wage workers. Black share of each of these jobs ranged between 11 per cent and 52 per cent of the national total.

The lowest black share in task assignments within firms was in such jobs as postmaster, engineer, buyer, commission salesman, lawyer, physician, dentist, pharmacist, architect, author, designer, accountant, editor. Black share of these jobs ranged from slightly in excess of half of 1 per cent to 3 per cent of the national total.

Some of the tasks assigned to blacks appear to be of a transitional nature; that is to say, the share of these jobs may as likely increase as decrease in the near future. In 1969, the black share was somewhat in the neighborhood of their share of total employment. Some of these jobs were telephone operator, elementary school teacher, office machine operator, sewing machine operator, typist, guard, barber, deliveryman, auto mechanic, construction and maintenance painter.

At the beginning of their wage laboring existence, members of the black population took on a well defined place in the division of labor within the External Labor Process. The tasks assigned were heavily weighted on the side of great physical exertion, high degree of danger, deadening monotony, minimal opportunity for arbitrary decision-making, significant distance from the levers of power and control over the work of others. These tasks coincided with the bottom rungs of the hierarchy of coordination and control in the firms, as well with low prestige among workers generally. But more important, they were for the most part tasks which were not specialized to the production of any particular commodity. These tasks were indeed general laboring activities, usable in the production of practically all types of commodities, and most amenable to incorporation into machine directed and controlled activities. Thus, the stage was set from the very beginning for imminent displacement of black wage workers in the constant quest by capitalist owners of firms for private profitability.

In spite of this ominous threat, black wage laborers have been a potent factor in the creation of material commodities in every industry throughout the land. The concentration of black workers has mirrored and reflected the different technologies within different industries. For example, in the personal service industries (hospitals, households, etc.) large numbers of unspecialized laborers are used. Hence, blacks tend to be concentrated more in these industries than in, say, aluminum refining, where the concentration of tasks have to do with chemical engineering.

We estimate that in 1965 blacks contributed a quantity of External Labor and a corresponding value of capital in the amount of $77 billions. Half, or $38 billions, represented unpaid labor. By 1981, we estimate that black External Labor and the corresponding value of black-produced capital amounted to $302 billions. Half, or $151 billions, constituted unpaid labor.

These are huge numbers. They constitute about 14 per cent of all capital produced within the nation; on the other hand, paid labor amounted to only 7 per cent of total capital produced.

On the basis of these numbers it would appear that we are dealing with a rate of exploitation of the black wage laboring population of about fifty per cent. This may be compared to an estimated rate of exploitation of the national wage laboring population of 40 per cent. In short, more than a normal share of profits is being extracted from the black population by capitalists who are almost exclusively non-black.

These results must have a devastating effect on the capability of the black population to reproduce itself. The rate of exploitation in the External Labor Process is but a mirror reflection of the extreme difficulty which this same population encounters as it attempts to survive on the basis of the rather meager shares of the material means of survival within the Internal Labor Process.

The black Internal Labor Process

The black Internal Labor Process is the set of institutional activities carried out by black people in black households to produce black human energy. Since human energy is an integral part of human beings and is carried within their persons, this institutional process is at the same time the process which produces the black human population.

Each black household contains a certain number of members of varying ages, genders, and other important characteristics. This membership configuration embodies the technology of Internal Labor, the production plan of the household, in the production of its members. This technology dictates the division of Internal Labor within each household, and establishes the operating parameters that relate the given household to all other black households.

An important characteristic of this process is that every last black household member must be produced. This simple fact leads to some interesting implications. Every member is an active participant and must be daily provided with a minimum quantity of food to replenish his/her vital energies and thus maintain the living status. In addition, other consumables deemed socially necessary must also be provided for consumption by every such member.

The using up, the consumption of consumer commodities by black household members, is one part of the activity of Internal Labor. The result is the production of black human energy congealed in the bodies and souls of black people. Production of black people entails two kinds of events – maintaining the living status of the existing survivors, and creating new human energy in the form of birthing of new offspring.

Over the relevant population formation period, say one hundred years, the total number of live births constitutes the potential population during the last year of the period. This potential consists of the surviving black population (those who are alive during the last year) and the stagnant black population (those who are not alive during the last year). The surviving population, in turn, consists of the latent black population (those who serve as replacements for the population at the beginning of the first year) and the active black population (those who constitute an increment over the latent population).

In sum, production of black human energy within the black Internal Labor Process requires the involvement of every last member of the black population. Implicit in the activity is the use of food and other consumables to create black human energy. But creation of black human energy entails the creation of the potential black population, consisting of the stagnant, the latent, and the active black population.

Black Internal Labor activity must go on relentlessly day by day, year by year. During any year, a given black household may experience death of one or more of its members. Such deaths may be replaced by births taking place during the same year. It is not generally the case that the replacement will come from the given family; more than likely the births which replace the deaths of the given family take place within a different black family. Herein lies one important interconnection between black families in the Internal Labor Process.

Black babies are born year in and year out. Some of them who survive play the social role of replacements for members of the black population who died. The replacement function, therefore, establishes a network of interdependence in the form of backward linkages in the serially sequential production of the black population.

Now these backward linkages cannot take place unless the material means of survival are available to those who act as replacements. Members of a given household can only get consumer goods through purchases in the consumer goods market; purchases require money; money is available to black employed workers through wages; and wages can be gotten only if the black worker is employed by a capitalist to directly or indirectly produce consumer goods.

A necessary condition, therefore, for the replacement function to take place is that the new babies who play this role must be born into households, each of which has at least one employed black member to provide the new babies with their material means of survival. Such households could be existing ones; or they could be new household formations.

The replacement function is the stabilizing part of the activity of Internal Labor. It provides for the maintenance of the black population at its initial numerical magnitude. As such, it ensures stability in black employment at least at its initial level.

Beyond the replacement function, Internal Labor Activity may provide for growth in the surviving black population over its initial level. We would assume that live black births which perform this role originate in newly formed households. But since they are survivors, this would imply that at least one member of each such household is employed. Hence, increment in black survivors and increment in black employment would vary directly under these conditions.

New household formation entails the yielding up of adult members from two existing households. These latter two adults, in turn, engage in the act of birthing a new black baby who plays the social role of black population growth. At least one of the new adult members must be employed by capitalists in the direct or indirect production of consumer goods. An increment in the surviving black population is therefore directly associated with an increment in the production of the material means of black survival.

New black household formations, increments in the surviving black population, increments in black employment, increments in black purchases of consumer goods, increments in black production of consumer goods – all of these are tightly interconnected events. For purposes of Internal Labor analysis, however, they point to the interconnections between black households in the cooperative sharing in the means of survival. These constitute the forward linkages which join existing black households to newly formed black households.

Finally, some of the new black live births will not survive the current year. They will therefore not become a part of the surviving black population. Indeed, they are what we call the stagnant population.

The stagnant births obviously cannot have access to any of the material means of survival. These births may originate out of both existing households and new household formations; however, such households would contain no employed adults, and therefore have no legitimate access to the material means of survival. Black unemployment and the size of the stagnant black population apparently are positively correlated.

Replacements, deaths out of current births, and growth in the surviving black population constitute the result of the activities of black people in the Internal Labor mode. Such a mode is a set of vivid moments of a people in the social act of creating the basis for the continuation of the population beyond the lifetime of its individual members.

The activities are at once using the material means of survival, birthing of babies, socializing them in the mores and traditions of the people, rearing them to adult maturity within the whole complex of social institutional relations which bind black people together whenever they function outside the markets and outside the External Labor Process. Education, religion, politics, art, music, recreation, family formation are some of the specific forms assumed by black Internal Labor.

At the beginning of the wage laboring period in 1965, the black surviving population stood at an estimated 22.5 million; the corresponding stagnant black population was estimated to be 23.1 million. Thus the potential black population was 45.5 million.

By 1981 the estimated black survivors had reached 27.7 million; the corresponding stagnant population was 25.9 million. Thus the potential black population was 53.6 million.

The average annual changes over the period 1965–81 were 175,000 stagnant births and 331,000 surviving births. Average annual births were 506,000 and average annual deaths were 300,000. Thus, growth in the surviving black population averaged 206,000 annually over the period.

Inputs of Internal Labor can be analyzed into two mutually exclusive components – paid, measured by the value of consumer goods purchased by black households; and the excess of Inputs of Internal Labor over the value of consumer purchases by black households. This latter may be referred to as accumulated black Internal Labor.

Internal Labor is an activity which comes to end. It results in the creation of human energy congealed in the material bodies of the potential black population. The potential black population may also be analyzed into two mutually exclusive components – the surviving population and the stagnant population.

We now have a direct way of relating the different components of Internal Labor with its material results. Potential black population corresponds to inputs of Internal Labor, surviving black population corresponds to black household consumer expenditures, and accumulated black Internal Labor corresponds to the black stagnant population.

In these value terms we estimate that in 1965 black households generated an input of Internal Labor of $77.2 billions. Half, or $38.6 billions, represented the value of consumer goods purchased by these households.

During 1981 we estimate that these magnitudes had undergone substantial change. Total input of Internal Labor amounted to an

Black wage labor and capital accumulation in the US

estimated $302.2 billions. Half, or $151 billions, represented the value of black household consumer purchases.

This overview of one of the most crucial institutional activities in which blacks participate in the political economy should give us a sense of the great contributions made by these people to the development of the national economy. They are enabled to purchase relatively little in the way of food and other material goods necessary for their survival. Yet, this very paucity of material goods forces them to adopt a technology of Internal Labor which generates a relatively large potential population.

At the same time, however, relatively small volume of material means of survival, coupled with relatively large potential population creation, results in a relatively large stagnant population. In other words, the cost in black human lives to sustain their existence is indeed quite exorbitant.

In any case, what goes on in the Internal Labor Process is a mirror of what takes place in the External Labor Process. After all, each of these labor processes is but a phase in the unified process of labor which sustains the political economy. The one presupposes the other in duration and intensity.

The unity of the two black labor processes

The black Internal Labor Process and the black External Labor Process are mirror reflections of each other. External Labor uses up black human energy and creates capital. Internal Labor uses up capital in the form of consumer goods and creates black human energy within the living bodies of black people. Neither type of labor can proceed for long without the other. They are mutually interdependent. Indeed, they are complementary opposites, manifesting the oneness of the act of laboring by the black human population in its quest for survival.

The one type of labor is exerted externally from the black population upon the earth or upon the previous products of that labor. It transforms black people into capital, under the direction and control and for the private property of non-black capitalists. The other type of labor is exerted internally to the black population itself. It transforms capital into black people, under their own direction and control and for their own private property or personal freedom. This latter, however, must respond to the requirements of the former.

Both types of labor are performed by the same black laboring population, but each is generated in the opposite direction. We have here a vivid example of a principle of conservation in action. That is to say, the quantity of black Internal Labor activity must equal the quantity of black External Labor activity. The one destroys the black laboring population; the other creates the black laboring population. Simultaneously, the one destroys capital; the other creates capital. What we have here is the conversion of black Internal Labor into black External Labor and conversely.

The two labor processes, taken together as a unity, are seen to follow a periodic cycle. This cycle undergirds the political economy. During one phase of the cycle black human energies are exhausted; during the succeeding phase those energies are revived. The amplitude and frequency of the labor cycle are dictated by the intensity and duration of exploitation of black people as reflected in the quickening pace of market activities, the necessary preconditions for labor to take place.

The end result of each complete cycle of black Internal and External Labor is a net change in all the elements which define the black wage laboring system within the general system of capitalist political economy in the United States. As a system it must continue *qua* that same system.

It can do this if (a) the black laboring population is reproduced as a black laboring population; (b) non-black capitalists who exploit black labor are reproduced as non-black capitalists; (c) material wealth produced by black labor is reproduced as capital.

The set of institutional activities which ensure the reproduction of the black wage laboring subsystem within the national capitalist system is the Process of Accumulation of Black Capital.

The Accumulation of Black Capital

The Process of Accumulation of Black Capital is the most fundamental of all the institutions of social reproduction of the black population. Indeed this institution presupposes the successful operation of all the others before it can make its own unique contribution. At the same time, all the other institutions presuppose

Black wage labor and capital accumulation in the US

the successful operation of accumulation before they can function properly. If there is a crisis in any of the other institutions, accumulation fails. Conversely, if accumulation fails, all the other institutions collapse forthwith. Successful operation of the Process of Accumulation of Black Capital is therefore both a necessary and a sufficient condition for the proper functioning of the process of reproduction of the black population.

The fundamental role of this process is to establish the effective conditions for the reproduction of the black wage labor system as a system of capitalist political economy. It accomplishes its task by transforming the results of all the other institutions of social reproduction into capital.

Certain necessary conditions must be satisfied before this process can function. The black Internal Labor Process must have already operated successfully; the black External Labor Process must have operated successfully. Unless these two sets of activities are completed, no black capital accumulation can ensue.

We have heretofore established the precondition that the effective execution of the two phases of labor is the simultaneous function of the two market mechanisms. Indeed, it is the unity of these two markets that provides to each of the labor processes the essential commodities which must be consumed in order to generate the corresponding phase of labor.

Finally, neither market can operate unless there exist members of a class of capitalists, each being a private owner of capital; and members of a class of black wage laborers, each being a private owner of human energy in the form of commodities. These two classes must confront each other in equal and voluntary interactions, alternately as buyers and sellers of commodities in the respective markets.

It goes without saying that the existence of a class of black wage laborers and a class of capitalists is a function of a long and protracted historical process.

In the case of the black wage laboring class, we traced that process from the origins in communal societies in Africa, through their involuntary migration across the Atlantic as articles of the infamous slave trade. We analyzed their exploitation under slave labor conditions for two and a half centuries. We studied their manumission from slavery and the installation of a system of feudal relations in which they were exploited under conditions of sharecropping labor in the southern states. Finally, we traced the historical process which expropriated them from the land and transformed them into a class of wage laborers by the latter half of the 1960s.

In all these developments we found no significant event which spun off a class of black capitalists. Hence, we come to the present day with black wage laborers generally interacting with non-black capitalists. This peculiar circumstance makes it a fact of life that black-produced capital is accumulated by non-black capitalists.

The non-black capitalists are the very same group who control the means of production in the national political economy. Their origins are well known and will not be the subject matter of this work.

Within the Process of Accumulation of Black Capital, two sets of commodities are accumulated. On the one hand, the black wage laboring population must be able to accumulate only that commodity whose production is under their control and private ownership. Their domain is black Internal Labor; the corresponding commodity is black human energy. The capitalist domain is black External Labor; the corresponding commodity is black-produced capital.

At the conclusion of every cycle of labor each capitalist must convert his capital into money. Only that part of capital which is equal in value to the wages paid out can be sold directly or indirectly to laborers. Hence, the part representing profits can be converted into money only by an exchange among capitalists themselves.

The interchange among capitalists is of fundamental importance. This is at the heart of the capital accumulation process. Each capitalist must be able to convert part of his profits into an amount of primary and intermediary commodities which replaces those used up in current production. In addition, each capitalist must be able to convert part of his profits into an increment of primary and intermediary commodities. In addition, each capitalist must be able to convert part of his profits into an increment of his money holdings. In addition each capitalist must be able to convert part of his profits into an increment to his inventory. Finally, each capitalist must be able to convert part of his profits into consumer goods for his own personal consumption.

We have monotonously spelled out the various conversions of

capital because this process does not seem to be well understood. These conversions of capital constitute what is generally meant by "investments." They involve sales by each capitalist to every other capitalist of the profits in the form of his particular capital; simultaneously, it involves the purchase by each capitalist of part of the profits of all the other capitalists. This complex arrangement of capitalist entanglement is thus seen to be a very delicate and sophisticated system of barter which can go awry with the slightest disturbance.

On the side of Internal Labor, each black wage laborer household is limited to a stock of money equal in value to the wages received from employment. But the money wage is also the limiting value of consumer goods which the black household may purchase in the market. These goods correspond to the surviving black population.

It must be recalled that the survivors are compounded of the latent black population and the active black population. The latent is replaced by surviving live births over the population formation period. But such replacements generally come from families other than the ones in which the deaths occurred.

Some of the survivors make up the active population; that is to say, the net additions to the survivors over and beyond the latent population. These originate out of the complex social arrangements involving new family formations. Two households yield up one adult member each to start the new household, which in turn gives birth to a new offspring. Repeated throughout the network of all black families, this process paves the way for a social process of the active population to become an integral part of the survivors.

Finally, part of the potential population is the stagnant element. Its demise is an integral part of the whole process of black population formation, originating out of the rate of exploitation of the black population as a whole.

These intricate networks of interdependent interactions which transpire within each of the two classes effectively result in the reproduction of black wage laborers as black wage laborers and the reproduction of non-black capitalists as non-black capitalists. Black wage laborers end up possessing commodities in the form of human energy only, if the consumer goods which they purchase on the market exhaust the entire sum of wages which they received in the market.

Black wage labor and capital accumulation in the US

The non-black capitalists end up possessing commodities in the form of capital, if all the wages they put out to workers return to them in the form of purchases of consumer goods by the workers.

The system of black wage labor needs another condition to ensure its continuity. The cycle of events must be joined once more. Black wage laborers as private owners of human energy must confront non-black capitalists as private owners of capital. The confrontation must be of a specific nature. It must, indeed, be a coming together in the market for black human energy.

So soon as this market relation is joined anew, the cycle of black wage laboring activities is restarted. This time, however, such activities are on a larger, smaller, or same scale as before. In capitalist political economy the acquisitive society is in force. An expanding capital out of profits is the order of the day. Some capitalists may be wiped out, others may expand, still others remain stationary. But on the whole, fewer and bigger capitalists come to dominate the scenery.

Even with the larger scale of labor, however, the ensuing employment of black workers may generally increase, but at an amount somewhat less than the increase in new family formations. In other words, unemployment, especially among new entrants into the black wage labor force, can well be an endemic characteristic of the capital accumulation process.

After all, over the long term more efficient use of resources is the motivation. But "efficiency" is to be understood in terms of "private profitability." Reductions in the wage bill over the long run for any given level of material production must be the end and aim of individual capitalists. For the system as a whole, the production of material commodities must move inevitably in the direction of requiring relatively less workers to produce any given volume. This is so because workers are receivers of paychecks, the basis of costs to the class of capitalists. Their function as producers of values is enhanced at the same time by the intensification of their labors by the use of increasing doses of intermediary commodities per worker. Displacement of wage receivers by capital accumulated from unpaid labor of the same wage receivers is one effective method for accomplishing this aim.

Black workers are particularly vulnerable to this aspect of capital accumulation. As the lowest paid among the general class of wage workers, greater exploitation and therefore greater profits are made upon their backs. This provides the possibility of larger increments of black capital being reinvested to displace the very black workers who created the capital in the first place.

Coupled with the greater rate of exploitation, blacks perform the types of generalized tasks which are much more easily amenable to replacement by machines. A double whammy thus afflicts these unfortunate souls. The greater is their contribution to the profitability of capitalist exploiters, the more difficult it becomes for them to sell their human energy, and therefore to get employment as time goes on.

We must now translate these events into actual numbers. They tell a dismal story from the vantage point of the black wage laboring population. They produce relatively more live babies than the national population as a consequence of the degree of exploitation to which they are subjected. But their surviving members are less than their birth proportions warrant.

This implies that the rate of exploitation of black wage laborers partly manifests itself in the disproportionate number of blacks who fail to show up in the surviving population. The material means of survival afforded them is too small in relation to the labors they must perform. They thus succumb at a relatively larger rate. The result is a disproportionately larger number of births, a direct response of the black Internal Labor Process to create anew the potential basis for the continuity of the black population.

During the period of the black wage labor system thus far, from 1965 to 1983, black births have averaged 500,000 annually. This is the annual increment in the potential black population and is also closely related to the annual increment in the black labor force. At the same time, black employment has averaged an annual increment of 145,000. We estimate that over this period the annual increment to the army of unemployed black workers has been 245,000, a figure closely related to the annual increment in the stagnant black population.

In value terms, non-black capitalists have been able to accumulate out of unpaid black labor an estimated $38.6 billions in 1965 and $151.1 billions in 1981.

These numbers are impressive. They bring into bold relief the fundamental economic problems faced by the black population. Under conditions of wage labor in the capitalist political economy of the US they exert labor of tremendous intensity to produce the material means of survival; correspondingly, they exert the same quantity of labor to produce themselves by using the material means of survival. But the legitimate rules of the game of capitalist political economy force them to yield up to non-black capitalists, without compensation, approximately half of the fruits of that labor.

What they receive as compensation is just sufficient to reproduce them as a black population of wage laborers. The remaining materials produced by them are accumulated as the private property of capitalists who form no essential part of the black population. Poverty – the absolute effect of the discrepancy between the quantity of black labor exerted and the meager quantity of the material means of survival which they receive – is cemented in the number of black people who succumb to death.

The surviving black population is merely the tip of the iceberg. Underlying these survivors, these warriors in the glorious struggle for existence and human historical continuity, is an equal number of dead black bodies who potentially could have taken their places among the living, but who are the victims of legal capitalist theft.

It cannot be overemphasized that these results are the legitimate outcomes of the nature of capitalist political economy insofar as they impact on the black population. That blacks are poverty stricken is therefore no mystery. Someone else is accumulating the material wealth which blacks produce. But these accumulators do this with all the force of law and custom enforced by the capitalist political state.

If an unemployed black mother steals a loaf of bread to feed her hungry children, she will be summarily carted off to prison as a thief. She is in consummate violation of the law of acquisition of capitalist private property; she has expropriated capitalist private property outside the nexus of the market relation.

If, on the other hand, a non-black capitalist steals the fruits of a black laborer's labor, such a capitalist is doing a magnanimous deed; he is not only providing employment to that black, but he is also contributing to the "national wealth" (no matter that it goes into his own private pocket). In this case, that capitalist acts in harmony with both the laws of the market (by which he acquired the ownership of the back laborer's human energy) and the laws of External Labor (the untrammelled right to use his private property to create materials for his private ownership and peaceable enjoyment). His particular brand of stealth is therefore legal. And it is the bounden duty of the Political State to protect that act.

Pity the poor black worker, therefore! He is in a most unenviable bind. Not only is the individual capitalist or capitalist firm with which he must deal in order to be able to exercise his labor a great adversary; he must also be subjected to the oppressive intervention of the Political State as enforcer of the rules under which that black worker may survive.

Within the context of capitalist political economy, private accumulation of capital is a legitimate act. It is buttressed by the fundamental nature of capitalist institutions of social reproduction. All the mechanisms conspire to make it impossible for a laborer to exert labor to directly satisfy her/his needs. That labor can only be legitimately exercised through the mediation of the market mechanisms through which the laborer cedes ownership of private proprietorship in her/his human energy and acquires ownership of a money wage. This wage is the outside limit to the quantity of the material means of survival which can be claimed by the worker. The difference between what her/his labor produces and what the wage can purchase represents the potential private capital accumulation of some capitalist. Legal theft is the name of the game; and all the force of law and custom and state power will be brought to bear upon those who would transgress against such stealth.

Black wage workers are caught up in this bind. Their very survival depends upon a curious relationship with the Political State. They blindly seek out the help of the Political State to shield them from the evils which are visited upon them from their relations with private capitalists. On the other hand, the very Political State from which they seek succor must carry out its basic functions with universal objectivity.

The role of the Political State

The fundamental role of the Political State in the black wage labor system is to maintain it as a system of capitalist political economy. This overriding responsibility of the state ramifies throughout the entire fabric of the economy, encompassing not only formal government agencies, but an intricate network of semigovernmental organizations and a wide range of interlocking private institutions as well.

The major strategy of the Political State is the preservation of capitalist private property. A substantial aspect of this strategy is the promulgation of the rules under which the institutions in the political economy must function.

The tactical approach is to be found in the specific acts of individuals who personally perform the necessary functions of enforcing the rules promulgated by the Political State. This requires the organization of a government bureaucracy, a group of people arranged into many agencies, each of which is responsible for a well-defined operation.

The extent and complexity of the government bureaucracy develop with the extent and degree of complexity of the political economy. The internal structures of these agencies, levels of operational responsibility, interrelationships between them, relations between them and other semi-public and private institutions are a few of the considerations one has to deal with in order to understand this apparently mysterious monster called government, the operational arm of the institution of the Political State.

What this amounts to is that the Political State must preserve the private property rights in commodity ownership of black wage laborers. It must also protect the private property rights of non-black capitalists in the ownership of commodities.

For example, in order for black wage laborers to acquire private property rights in consumer goods owned by capitalists, they must do so only under consumer commodity market relations with those capitalists. Thus, one important function of the Political State is to promulgate and enforce rules governing consumer commodity market behavior. Blacks cannot, under these rules, expropriate those consumer goods without giving up an equal value of money in exchange. And the coming together of the two parties and the final terms of the exchange must not be coerced, but must be the voluntary expression of their individual wills.

Similarly, in order for non-black capitalists to acquire private property rights in ownership of human energy owned by blacks, they must do so only under relations of the market for black human energy. Thus, another function of the Political State is to promulgate and enforce the rules of behavior in the market for black human energy. Non-black capitalists cannot expropriate the human energy of black workers without giving up to them an equal money in exchange. And the coming together of the two parties and the final terms of exchange agreed upon must not be coerced, but must be based on the voluntary expression of their independent wills.

Once non-black capitalists have acquired the human energy formerly owned by black wage laborers, they must have the peace and freedom to use it according to their own discretion and to own privately the material results of such use. In particular, if they choose to use black human energy to produce capital, then the specific way in which they use that energy and the intensity of its use are their prerogatives. In addition, the capital is the private property of the non-black capitalists.

The Political State must see to it that the black worker does not try to exercise so-called constitutional guarantees of free speech, freedom of religion, and the right to assembling whenever he exerts labor in the capitalist's workplace. For in the relations between black workers and non-black capitalists in the External Labor Process, the exertion of labor by the worker is nothing more nor less than the specific method by which the capitalist consumes the black human energy, which, in this relation, belongs to the capitalist, not to the worker. Civil rights of the black worker have no standing here. It is indeed the rights of private proprietorship of the capitalist that hold sway.

Here is political irony. A system based on equality between black wage laborers and non-black capitalists in market relations and the sanctity of private property in commodity ownership (civil rights of the worker), spawns the legitimate superiority of capitalist and subordination of black laborers in the External Labor Process.

Once black wage laborers have acquired private ownership of consumer goods formerly owned by non-black capitalists, they must have the peace and freedom to use those goods according to their own discretion and to own privately the results of such use. In particular, if they choose to use consumer goods to produce black human energy, then the specific way in which they use those goods and the intensity of their use are the black worker's prerogatives. In addition, the black human energy, in so far as it is a commodity, is the private property of the black worker, not of the capitalist.

It is in this sphere of activity that the Political State must guarantee the private proprietorship of the black wage laborer in his human energy. But since he carries this energy as part of his bodily make-up and spiritual essence, his civil rights in his own person must be guaranteed by the Political State.

There is some irony here. In practice, the Political State's protection of the civil rights in this sphere generally amounts to arbitration between two or more black workers. Very little, if anything substantive, is done about capitalist encroachment upon the rights of black workers.

It appears that in this sphere the Political State plays a neutral role in its ministrations of justice and in the settlement of disputes. On the contrary, the very process of socialization of black babies and children must systematically produce specific types of human energy commodities. Black human carriers of that energy must be sufficiently disciplined to bend their individual wills voluntarily to conform to the rules of capitalist political economy.

It is not too difficult to understand, therefore, that the Political State must encroach upon the interactions of black people, one with another, in the Internal Labor Process. Thus, a number of activities come under the scrutiny and intervention of the government bureaucracy and its coteries of semi-public and private institutions. Family formations, births, deaths must be done legitimately. Education – both public and private – must conform to established standards. The unemployed, paupers, handicapped, orphans, elderly, criminal must be provided for. Political activity, recreation, literature, art, music, religion, public expression must not be seditious. Books, newspapers, magazines, radio, television, telephone must constantly inform the ignorant about current changes in the rules of the capitalist game.

It should now be clear that all of these practical functions of the Political State can be summarized in its role as arbiter of the Process of Accumulation of Black Capital. The Political State imposes the legal, moral, and physical force that binds black wage laborers and their household members under the two fundamental market relations. This ensures that capitalists will have the legitimate right and effective opportunities to commandeer black human energy as their private property, to be used for the purpose of creating capital for the private benefit and purposes of the capitalists. At the same time these market relations set the legitimate terms of trade under which black wage laborers acquire the material means of survival of their household members.

Like Vulcan riveting Prometheus to the rock, the Political State forces the black workers, against their natural will, to cede their right to labor and their right to the fruits of that labor to an alien people. It is no wonder, therefore, that the penitentiaries overflow with black criminals, a significant number of whom are in violation of the market principle. They have stolen the proverbial loaf of bread of the non-black capitalists; they have committed a cardinal sin against the god of capital.

All the time an opposition of the black wage laborers continues apace against the binding and oppressive force of these market relations. The opposition is precisely in the form of labor, the alternating pulsations of the phases of black External and black Internal Labor. This exertion is a continuing attempt to escape from the bonds of market oppression by creating the material means of survival and using whatever is available to create anew the black population. But, alas, such labor can only be exerted within the social boundaries of the market forces imposed by the Political State.

From the standpoint of the black population, the problem of escape is aggravated by the fact that the non-black capitalists, with the active participation and acquiescence of the Political State, control the terms of External Labor. In addition, the Political State dictates the "standards" of Internal Labor. Finally, the ravages of capitalist-controlled External Labor upon the bodies and souls of black workers establish the effective quantity of Internal Labor which must be generated by blacks.

In general, then, the opposing acts of black labor, attempting to dissolve the bonds of market relations, are confined within limits set by capitalists, in consort with the Political State. The system of black wage labor exploitation thus operates within bounds independent of the deliberate will of the black population, in so far as that black population conforms to the rules of the capitalist political economy. Even the very organizations which they create to wage their political, economic and social battles become tools for keeping them within the bounds of capitalist exploitation. After all, these organizations must be themselves legitimate entities.

The black bootstrap has been snatched away from black hands. Alas, they cannot pull themselves up!

Black wage labor and capital accumulation in the US

We must not lose sight of the fact that the activities of the capitalist Political State simulate the production and accumulation of capital. Wage laborers are employed, capital is used up by these laborers in the act of laboring, capital used up is replaced by purchases from private business firms, and capital of the types which define the special character of the External Labor Process of the Political State is accumulated.

The specific things which the political state produces are the arming and deployment of military and police forces to provide a base of operations that is secure from foreign encroachment as well as from domestic disturbance; the minimum sale of its services and products to the private sector, equal in value to the wages it pays out to government workers (government taxation of business); purchase of capital from private firms in an amount equal to the profitability of its operations (government expenditures for goods); redistribution of wage incomes among both employed and unemployed wage laborers (providing relief assistance to households with unemployed members); etc.

For black people, these functions of the Political State have been considerable. Black unemployment has been vicious. For black teenagers it is almost total; the same is true for the elderly blacks. Prime age blacks experience more than their proportionate share. Black women, particularly those without husbands but with children, are devastated by this condition. Blacks are significant tenants of jails, hospitals, rest homes; a significant number of employed blacks receive wages which cannot satisfy minimal food, housing, clothing requirements.

These conditions require some sort of state subvention through its wage redistribution programs. Aid to dependent children, food stamps, other forms of government transfers are made available to a disproportionate number of blacks. But these programs are designed at such meager levels, and are manipulated according to the immediate needs of the Political State, that blacks are made to undergo a most degrading and humiliating experience when receiving such aid.

On the other hand, the Political State has been a kind of last resort for black employment. Indeed, governments at all levels employ about 20 per cent of employed blacks. It doesn't matter that the overwhelming majority of these are in the lowest paying jobs and performing tasks that are not high on the prestige hierarchy. Orderlies and practical nurses in the hospitals, maids and janitors in government offices, postal clerks, elementary teachers are among these tasks. In recent years the military has taken its good share of black youth, thus helping to delay the time when fully one hundred per cent of black teenagers will be unemployed.

During the period when blacks were making the transition from sharecroppers to wage laborers, the Political State functions were resident in semi-autonomous southern state and local government bureaucracies. Official, semi-official, and private gendarmes ran riot in inflicting physical violence upon recalcitrant members of the black population.

From the beginning of the Great Migration in the second decade of the twentieth century to the end of the 1930s ku klux klan threats and intimidation and outright murder were the common mode of enforcement of the rules of the Political State.

After 1940 official organs of the local governments took over. The sheriffs and the courts in the southern states and local communities came together in reckless conspiracies to officially indict, try, and convict large numbers of young black men on trumped up charges of rape of white women. The disproportionate number of blacks who went to the electric chair and the inordinate number of documented cases of police brutality consumed practically the entire time and resources of the southern branches of the newly formed NAACP.

On the northern scene where black wage laboring was making a major foothold, similar forms of state power were visited upon the black population. Officially sanctioned restricted covenant agreements which denied blacks the right to live where they pleased, police brutality, vagrancy arrests, murder by white police and white working-class mobs typified some of the ways in which state power operated to keep blacks in line.

It was not until the 1960s, when the wage labor transition was approaching consummation, that the national Political State began to take a hand in formally ceding to blacks the rights and privileges necessary for wage laboring status.

Many of the remnants of sharecropping existence were either wiped off the books or were rendered inoperative by the primacy of federal statutes and regulations which had for at least one hundred years applied to the non-black workers.

The millennium had not arrived. Yet, the mere fact of acquiring the status of a *bona fide* wage laborer meant the acquisition of the rights of private proprietorship of one's ability to work and its concomitant civil rights to one's self. In contrast to the former black existence and black relationship to the Political State an aura of euphoria blanketed the black community. Little did these people realize that a new set of shackles would bind them to a more efficient mode of exploitation. It wasn't long before the realization swept across the black community. The dream died when the capitalist Political State of the United States surrendered in shame in the War on Poverty during the 1970s.

Whatever is their fate, black people have been listening to some of their numbers espousing a strange policy that they should integrate themselves into the national political economy on a color-blind basis. The essence of such proposals is for the black population urgently to spin off a class of black capitalists who would usurp the role now played by non-black capitalists in the accumulation of black capital. Presumably, black capitalists would preserve the national character of black wealth.

No matter what the distribution effects, nor the prospective class cleavage within what is now a homogeneous wage working black population, progress would be inevitable, so they say. And we shall see.

Formation of a class of black capitalists

Prior to the turn of the twentieth century there was practically no possibility of a class of black capitalists emerging as a reality in the North American scene. Under the slave regime, of course, this would have been a total anomaly. With the demise of slavery and the introduction of the sharecropping system slight possibilities may have existed; however, the practical opportunities available to blacks to acquire capital were exceedingly limited.

The era of transition of the black sharecropper into a wage laborer, commencing in earnest sometime during the second decade of the twentieth century, spawned a series of events which made possible the simultaneous development of a black capitalist class. These potential black capitalists possibly could have tried to emulate some of their non-black counterparts who were actively engaged in amassing primitive capital on the backs of the black

Black wage labor and capital accumulation in the US

cropper as well as upon the backs of the new black entrants into the wage laboring class.

The opportunities available for amassing a stock of primitive black capital were many. However, they practically resolved themselves into theft of sufficiently large tracts of land from black independent subsistence land owners; or conspiring with state and federal governments to acquire, free of charge, ownership of public lands; or the strategic use of merchant capital to siphon off a portion of the cotton produced by black sharecroppers; or the use of merchant capital to steal from the new black wage workers part of the excess of their wages over the cost of their food supply; or to use church and other black institutions to gather up any loose sacrificial monies designed for future burials or other contingencies.

The problem with that strategy for primitive capital accumulation by would-be black capitalists is that the field was already usurped by both established and developing non-black capitalists. The competition was formidable. Nevertheless, a few black businesses got a foothold during this period and survived to become *bona fide* capitalist enterprises.

By the middle of the 1960s a few insurance companies, a publishing company, a meat processing factory, a beauty products concern, an entertainment conglomerate, a supermarket chain, and a few other black owned businesses stood out as the elite among a relatively small group of firms which operated with the leading national technology of their respective industries. None, however, was of a size to make the *Fortune* second five hundred industrials, nor the fifty largest in banking, insurance, finance, transportation, communication, public utility, retailing.

The first official national census of black owned business in 1969 identified some 200,000 such firms. Only 32,000 employed paid workers. Among the latter, a mere handful of less than 3,000 reported more than ten employees. A closer scrutiny of these firms indicated that the employees of the majority of these firms were employed on a part-time or sporadic basis. Of 65,000 live bodies claimed as employees, no more than 20,000 full time equivalents really had jobs.

These 3,000 firms were concentrated in retail and wholesale (37 per cent), selected service (24 per cent), manufacturing (15 per cent), and finance/insurance/real estate (12 per cent). They contributed an estimated $250 millions to the gross national product.

By 1981 no significant change could be discerned in the number and size of these few black owned business firms. The future prospect for growth is also rather dismal. Monopoly capital has a stranglehold on the leading sectors of the economy. Any breakthrough must involve winning a desperate struggle against some of the most powerful business giants that have ever functioned upon the face of the earth. And today, they do in fact function with reckless abandon throughout the entire globe.

Owners of these black firms, joined by an estimated 2,000 independent black professionals who own fairly good investments in the nation's corporations, constitute the sum total of the class of capitalists. Thus, about 15,000 members of this group's households are the sum total of the black middle-class – the alleged black bourgeoisie.

This class fades into insignificance within the totality of the black population. It is no wonder then that many pseudo-analyses have erroneously classified blacks at the higher end of the black wage distribution as being members of the "middle class." Capitalism's characteristic signature is an extremely wide and dispersed distribution of wage payments among its wage laborers. Black workers are no less subject to this phenomenon than any other group of workers.

Analytically, then, one may completely dismiss the existence of a black capitalist class. Essentially, it is the interaction of the entire black population in its role as a class of wage laborers with the entire class of national non-black capitalists that is of moment.

The black wage labor system operates within the larger US economy as an integral part thereof. In this system blacks interact with non-black capitalists and the extremely large class of non-black wage laborers.

And then there is the rest of the world.

Interactions between black wage laborers and the rest of the world

The milieu in which the black wage labor system is imbedded is the national capitalist political economy of the United States. As such, black wage laborers interact directly with the national class of capitalists. Nothing new need be added to this account except to remind ourselves that the iron laws which govern the system as a whole must likewise operate with telling force on the black system. However, they operate with special historical impact.

Within the larger context there stands a numerically staggering class of non-black wage workers. Black wage workers are in direct contact with these people in all facets of their economic life.

In the national market for human energy, black and non-black workers come into competition for a limited number of jobs offered by the same class of capitalists. Such competition does degenerate into physical and mental conflict, sometimes bordering on working-class fratricide.

From the very beginning of their wage laboring existence, blacks were used as pawns in the profit-making game by northern capitalists. They were used as scabs, strike breakers, general threats to strikes in progress, or threats to the security of jobs and wages of non-black workers.

This first meeting of the two segments of the working class was not a propitious one. But blacks couldn't care less. Non-black workers had put blacks into auxiliary pseudo-unions in the south. In many northern unions they were not even allowed to join. The general market for human energy thus began in conflict between these two segments of the working class and still continues to this day under even greater pressures of the huge army of unemployed workers of both groups.

Some abatement of the conflict in this market setting has emerged out of some national developments. Beginning after World War I, all black or heavy majority black unions were organized in post office, railroad sleeping car service, red cap service, hospitals. Blacks began playing a role of growing importance in a number of other unions which came into existence out of the organizing drives of the CIO during the 1930s. Some of these were steel, auto, meat packing, tobacco processing. Highly visible black membership and black leadership, together with the changing residential patterns, were instrumental in pushing some blacks into positions of decision-making in shops, on the boards of locals, on executive committees of internationals, and even in the inner temples of the national federations. In this latter area, blacks have become deeply involved in running political action and civil rights activities.

The upshot of these interactions, however, is that much conflict still remains. The practice of non-black capitalists reserving the lowest pay for black workers has tended to yield additional fuel to the fires of psychological separation of the two groups. Money talks; and less money conjures up in the eyes of others visions of inferiority of ability and effort.

In the External Labor Process blacks have been definitely relegated to a few special tasks in the division of labor within the firm. The specialty of these tasks is precisely that they are generalized tasks, pretty common to all branches of industry. Janitors, maids, orderlies, ironers, truck drivers, miscellaneous clerks are some of these tasks. These just happen to be the specialties which are deemed to be rather low down the prestige hierarchy. Hence, objective conditions persist which could be rationalized as inferior social ability in the eyes of the non-black workers.

In spite of this, External Labor is still a paragon of social production. Cooperation among all workers regardless of specialty is the *sine qua non* of this process. Furthermore, cooperation among workers in the different firms which form a part of the serially coordinated production process of a single commodity binds black workers to non-black workers across the entire economy in very important ways. Joint struggles against the oppressive tendencies of capital in the work place and within an industry help to forge a bond between all workers.

The market for consumer goods also forces a separation of black wage workers from all other workers. Greater concentrations of blacks in the low wage jobs mean the smaller purchases of non-food goods. Other workers witness blacks purchasing smaller quantities of housing, schooling, health care, transportation, recreation, and other socially requisite materials. In addition, even if blacks purchase the same quantities of food, the nutritional quality is much less.

The social significance of all this is that the greater part of black wages must be used to purchase food, an item without which they could not survive. Relatively small shares of the incomes of blacks are left over to purchase other items. The contrast with non-black wage workers is obvious. Two identifiable segments of the consumer goods market get delineated in terms of the two subsets of workers. This provides a visible manifestation for a rationale of inferiority of the black consumer goods market operator.

The Internal Labor Process has thus far been one in which black wage laborers produce themselves in great isolation from non-black wage laborers. The fundamental act of creation of the babies who form the basis of the population is done separately in black wage laborers' households and separately in non-black wage laborers' households. Two separate surviving populations result. Intermarriage has been relatively insignificant. Over the last decade it has increased in incidence, but it does not yet appear that there will be an avalanche of such unions taking place in the near future.

An integral aspect of separate birthing of babies is the whole complex set of social activities involved in nurturing them, recreating them, instilling in them the morals of the community, generally rearing them to full maturity, and socializing them to the conditions of existence in capitalist political economy.

These things have thus far been carried out in separate ways by the two groups. Public schools remain segregated, possibly as a consequence of black consumption of the most dilapidated housing in segregated neighborhoods. Religion is practiced in separate churches, temples, synagogues and even in radically different ways within the same denominations. Recreational facilities remain in the respective neighborhoods. Political activity is based on blocs of voters within each of the two communities. The literature, art, music, scholarship of each group take on distinctive flavors and interpretations.

The Process of Capital Accumulation segregates the two groups of workers. Lower pay for blacks and the consequent lower level of consumer goods purchasable are visible indices of the higher rate of exploitation of black wage workers. This takes a differential toll on blacks in terms of relatively greater number of deaths, which is the same thing as lower rates of survival.

But the greater rate of exploitation of black workers implies a greater rate of transformation of their unpaid labor into capital. This further means the possibility of relatively greater displacement of black workers from the employed labor force. Thus blacks form a disproportionately larger part of the army of the unemployed and of the subset of paupers within this group.

Within the Internal Labor Process, the relatively low level of goods available for consumption by black workers is a visible indication of the greater intensity of labor which must be exerted to overcome the inertial element. Relatively greater numbers of births within the black households must help to make up for those who fall victim to death.

Greater unemployment, more frequent deaths, and the baggage of related malaise they bring with them place blacks in a peculiar position relative to their fellow workers. The Political State has to intervene to provide some modicum of survival materials to the black unemployed and paupers. As we have seen, it does so by redistributing black wages and making minimal and humiliating handouts to the officially proclaimed black paupers. On the other hand, non-black workers are encouraged to believe that it is their taxes which are making the giant share of support of the black poor. Enmity and uninformed selfishness become the separator.

We need not go any further. The activities of individual capitalists in their employment policy, their assignment of tasks in the division of External Labor, and the extent of expropriation of black unpaid labor have continued to forge a dichotomy among two essentially similar subsets of the general working class.

Black workers see these events as racism on the part of non-black workers. They interpret them as the machinations of evil, racist white workers who will visit the pauper's status on black people, and in the last analysis will maim and kill them and blast them into oblivion.

But we should know from the long recitation of events which we have thus far presented, that the apparently racist activities of non-black workers are nothing but the institutional imprints of the system of political economy using these latter workers as the specific instrumentalities of working-class fragmentation to render them ineffective in their common struggle for survival.

The question of moment is concerned with where will all of this lead. A conscious construction of common bonds of interests between the two groups of workers or a widening of the rift between them are two alternatives which seem to be equally possible in the future.

8 The role of black Americans in the social reconstruction of the future

Black Americans have come a long historical way. From primordial beginnings on the African soil, perhaps some three million years ago, they evolved as isolated members of human families, with few interconnections outside of their immediate households.

At some critical juncture in their evolution they yielded up the exclusive dominion of family life to the supremacy of the clan. Hand in hand with this development came the effective transformation of isolated individual family labor into clan social labor. The communal social revolution was consummated by this earth-shaking event.

Members of the society now labored in common to satisfy their individual and social needs. No outside human agents dictated the terms on which they could exercise their labors, nor fixed their quantitative shares in the material result of that labor. Only the natural proclivities of the larger earth environment presented challenges to be overcome as they went about their daily chores. A classless society of black men, women, and children thereby subsisted in dynamic harmony with the African earth.

This harmony was not to endure forever. At a certain juncture in world history this African communal existence was disrupted by the coming of a band of alien invaders from across the seas. In conspiracy with some native African merchant marauders and feudal satraps, the aliens enslaved the communalists, shipped them across the ocean sea as living cargo in the stinking holds of their ships, and made them to work the plantations of the Americas for the private benefits of other alien masters.

This transformation of the black African communalists into black American slaves required three necessary conditions for its successful completion. The black communalists themselves were appropriated as the private property of the aliens; the aliens seized private ownership and control of the slaves' Internal Labor Process; and the aliens seized private ownership and control of the slaves' External Labor Process.

But these three conditions were not sufficient. In order to insure the unified and uninterrupted exertion of both phases of slave labor, the personal iron will of the aliens had to dictate to the slave all the conditions under which labor would take place. These conditions effectively set the legitimate rate of exploitation of black slaves at fully one hundred per cent of the fruits of their labors.

In time, the black slaves were personally freed; but they now entered upon a new existence as landless peasant sharecroppers. Three necessary conditions defined their new social status. The cropper was personally free, the alien landlords seized ownership and control of the cropper's External Labor Process, and the alien landlords seized control (if not outright ownership) of the cropper's Internal Labor Process.

But these conditions were not sufficient. The uninterrupted and unified exertion of both phases of a cropper's labor required the "voluntary" acquiescence of the cropper in an agreement which bound him/her for life to landless status upon the land. This agreement established the legal basis for the alien landlord to aggrandize the major portion of the fruits of the black cropper's labor, fixing the rate of exploitation somewhere between fifty and one hundred per cent.

In recent years the black sharecroppers liberated themselves from the shackles of the sharecropping system and were transformed into wage laborers. Three necessary conditions defined this new social arrangement. The black wage laborer became personally free; the black wage laborer seized control (and ownership) of the Internal Labor Process, and alien capitalists seized ownership and control of the External Labor Process.

These conditions were not sufficient. The uninterrupted and unified exertion of labor required voluntary submission of both capitalists and black wage laborers to market rules. These rules fixed the legitimate terms under which blacks may have the opportunity to exert External Labor; these rules also fixed the quantity of the material fruits of black External Labor which would be returned to them for their own personal use. Therefore, these

Black Americans in the social reconstruction of the future

market rules effectively set the legal rate of exploitation of the black wage laborer somewhere between zero and fifty per cent.

These dramatic historic transformations of the black population point to progressive trends in the conditions of these people. They were enslaved in the beginning; but they won their freedom. Personal freedom persisted throughout the next two succeeding social revolutions. In the last transformation, in addition to their personal freedom, they also won control over their Internal Labor Process.

However, they still have no power to make decisions about the quantity, extent, and results of Internal Labor. As a matter of fact, their so-called voluntary market decisions place them in a situation where the very nature and extent of their Internal Labor (which they own and control) must respond in lock-step fashion to the ravages inflicted upon them in the External Labor Process (which they do not own nor control).

The future course is clear. Members of the black wage laboring population must, at all costs, maintain possession of their personal freedom. This is the *sine qua non* of their future existence.

They must also maintain ownership, and strive for complete control, of the Internal Labor Process. The quantity, extent, and result of this phase of their labor must be grounded in the principle of the creation of a black laboring population which is molded in the true spirit of human perfectibility.

They must also make a quantum leap forward in their historical condition by seizing ownership and control of the External Labor Process. No longer should an alien class dictate the extent, nature, and result of the phase of labor which produces the material means of their survival. These decisions should be theirs and theirs alone.

These three conditions are necessary, but far from sufficient, for total liberation from the exploitative machinations of capitalist reproductive relations. Indeed, if there is to be a synchronous handshaking interaction between the two phases of labor, performed for the total interests of the black population, then black people must push into oblivion the market institutions which now fix the terms of their exploitation.

Market principles are the epitome of capitalist private property relations. These principles must give way to assignment of tasks in the External Labor Process based on the personal talents which inhere in each black individual. At the same time, each individual member of the black population must receive an amount and kind of material goods based on his/her own individual needs. The new principles of distribution, however, must be tempered by the collective social goals, democratically arrived at.

In short, the future programme for black Americans requires the demise of the capitalist form of exploitation of their labor. It also entails the construction of a new social order based on personal freedom, equal opportunity and the inalienable right to participate in the creation of the material means of survival, and the effective right to acquire quantities and types of the material means of survival based purely on individual need.

This is heady stuff. At the present time black people constitute less than 12 per cent of the US surviving population. They operate in an environment in which the non-black members of the wage working class are rather backward in terms of the conscious understanding of common interests which bind them indelibly to their black wage laboring brothers and sisters.

Blacks also subsist under rules promulgated and enforced by a not too friendly, if not totally repressive, political state.

Furthermore, a good number of blacks still hold out the hope of surviving with dignity within the bowels of the present national capitalist order. They believe that in time they will be able to achieve capitalist status; or at second best, they will penetrate the upper levels of the wage distribution. More schooling, especially on the higher levels; affirmative action stimuli into the upper reaches of the hierarchy of control within the division of labor; more intensive involvement in capitalist party political affairs; stepping up the pace of establishment of black business enterprises – these and other pathways are relied on to bring about the millennium within the existing capitalist social relations.

Today, blacks are still exploited to a greater degree than their non-black counterparts. Average wage payments, and consequently average acquisition of the material means of survival place blacks at about 70 per cent of the living standard of non-blacks. The greater rate of exploitation is linked in a very important way to the greater rate of unemployment of blacks. Blacks experience greater rate of decay of the potential population; that is to say, they die off much more rapidly.

These and other factors may present obstacles to the black

Black Americans in the social reconstruction of the future

struggle for freedom. Yet, the developing realities of black life in the United States may help to paint a clearer picture of the future.

The two great revolutions – slavery to landless peasantry, landless peasantry to wage laboring – were won by blacks themselves. There is still a universality of thought, even among blacks, that somehow blacks have been passive receptacles into which historical change has flowed. This notion dies hard.

Many blacks believe that it was northern capitalist armed might which gave the decisive death blow to slavery. The stimulus for this military campaign, it is believed, originated out of the moral indignation of leading abolitionists, aided and abetted by the interests of the northern capitalist class.

An integral part of this type of thinking is that revolutions which come from the downtrodden are struck by heroic deeds of brave individuals. Black slave revolts did occur, but they were soon put down. The heroes were there, but alas they did not succeed. In the case of the destruction of the feudal sharecropping relations, absolutely nothing is said about individual black heroes. As a matter of fact, the black sharecropping migrant – that revolutionary worker on the road toward social transformation – was believed to be the source of black urban problems.

While there is a modicum of truth in all this, it is nevertheless a most incomplete way of looking at the facts. It was a result of black efforts throughout their history that brought on revolutionary changes. The heroes are the nameless millions of men, women, and children – all black – whose births, and lives, and deaths now enrich the American soil.

If there is one theme which dominates this work it is precisely that the liberating force of all exploited classes in history is the exertion of human labor. Labor is the critical activity which makes a people's survival possible. It creates both the material means of survival and the people themselves. The fact that it has existed under exploitative pressures, generally manifested in the characteristic distribution mechanisms, is precisely the dynamic which brings about change in society.

The greater the degree of exploitation, the greater must be the exertion of human labor if the population is to survive. But the greater the exertion of human labor, the greater is the opportunity for increased levels of exploitation. The one feeds upon the other. But all the time, the explosive character of human labor must reach a magnitude that defies any distributional mechanisms to contain it. This is the fundamental nature of the internal contradiction which inheres in any social order.

The problem for blacks has been that in the cases of the two social revolutions which they won through their own labor efforts, on each occasion an opportunistic alien ruling class stood at the ready to ensnare the new black laboring class into its tentacles and to impose a new exploitative labor system upon them. So was it in the case of the southern landlords after the freeing of the black slaves. So too was it in the case of the capitalists at the liberation of the black sharecropper.

At the consummation of both black social revolutions, no black ruling class was spawned by the political and economic upheavals. Blacks continued as a homogeneous working class, but with their African identity remaining intact. The essential meaning of this is that in no important sense can we separate out African origin (the only sensible interpretation of what people mean by "race") and class status of black Americans. Blacks have been, throughout the American experience, of African (black) origin and simultaneously a working class – black slaves, black sharecroppers, black wage laborers.

The two great social revolutions were won at times when the non-black working class was of a different historical mold than their black counterparts. Black slaves existed in the same real time interval alongside non-black landless peasants; black sharecroppers carried on their labors in the same real time interval alongside non-black sharecroppers, non-black landless peasants, non-black independent peasants, and non-black wage workers.

There is no way now, however, to isolate the class of black wage laborers from the class of non-black wage laborers. The social division of labor manifested in co-operation between black and non-black wage workers across the nation, and the process of capital accumulation itself, have erased any important objective distinguishing characteristics of the two segments of the working class.

In the near future we project that black survival rates will approach that of the nation as a whole. It should be obvious that the start of the black wage labor system represented a significant decline in the rate of exploitation, which should translate into

Black Americans in the social reconstruction of the future

increased survival. Already, the blackening of the larger cities across the nation previews this impending event.

Finally, blacks have not yet exercised what modicum of personal freedom they possess to forge more formal relationships with the African nations of their origin. Haltingly, they are increasing their individual contacts with specific African nations and African nationals. In recent years they have even tried to bring some of their concerns to the Organization of African Unity and to the organs of the United Nations. In short, blacks are becoming more conscious of the international impacts of their struggle for freedom.

The social revolution is now in progress. It is proceeding apace in step with the rate of capital accumulation upon the backs of the black population. Stolen black labor, transformed into non-black material wealth, spells the physical death of black people. But that selfsame capital signals the extent of the corresponding intensification of black Internal Labor which is being exerted to overcome the ravages of death.

Inherent in the Internal Labor is the source for creation of a surplus black population over and beyond the exploitative needs of capital. This is reflected in the growing absolute magnitude of unemployed blacks who represent the "freeing" up of blacks from the binding forces of the capitalist market mechanisms. In short, unemployment among the members of the black population signals the growing liberation of black people from direct capitalist exploitative mechanisms.

It therefore becomes extremely urgent that a black "safety net" be installed by blacks themselves to capture these unemployed black workers to be used to exert black labor in the total interests of black people. No more can blacks afford to have the revolution betrayed by alien aggrandizers. The only issue at stake is to determine the nature of that black "safety net."

The principles governing the nature of the net were laid out above. The net must preserve black personal freedom. The net must give to the freed black households complete control over their Internal Labor. The net must give to the freed black households complete control over their External Labor.

This latter characteristic of the net is the most decisive change of status which the social revolution requires. In practical terms, this condition requires that the freed black households devise their own system for the creation of their material means of survival.

Black Americans in the social reconstruction of the future

First and foremost, both phases of labor must serve the production of the most elementary material means of survival — their continuing food requirements. At the present time, this works out to about twenty million metric tons annually, and will increase by an annual amount in the foreseeable future by about 375,000 metric tons. The composition in terms of different types of food and the corresponding nutritive substances was implicit in some of our previous discussions. Food can be produced only by the exertion of External Labor upon the pristine earth. Common ownership of land thus becomes indispensable.

Land ownership is fairly well understood throughout the black community. However, with the exception of the Republic of New Africa, most blacks are ambiguously committed to the concept. To many of them landed existence conjures up the old sharecropping days and the associated backwardness of the rural life. This aspect of the program has to be made an important consciousness raising activity of highest priority. Acquisition of common ownership of the three million acres now privately owned by blacks, and the common acquisition of more land in the continental United States are essential parts of this program.

Food production for meeting the continuing requirements of the black population is absolutely essential. Beyond this, organizing to produce the other material requirements of the black population must hinge on what is done about the food question. Implementation of the food program in the right way sets the necessary basis for the production of other material means of survival.

In any case, the organization and implementation of the production of the black people's food supply must begin with the material means of production — the land — collectively owned by all black people. The second requisite is to marshall the subjective element out of the increasing number of blacks who form part of the reserve army of the unemployed in the United States.

Let's be clear about whom we speak. Unemployed blacks are not to be confused with those who have been recently subjected to indefinite lay-offs from their jobs. These latter are victims of the ever recurring cycles of External and Internal Labor and are associated with the ailments of specific firms or industries within the political economy. The fundamental element of the unemployed blacks with which we are immediately concerned consists primarily of those who, upon newly entering the wage labor force do not ever get employed. They cannot be associated with the problems of any specific firms or industries. They are the victims of the national process of accumulation of black-produced capital. They are the living human manifestations of the internal contradictions of the capitalist political economy.

It is indeed these youthful blacks who join the reserve army of the unemployed at the rate of half a million annually. How to organize these youths for productive existence in the new social order presents the great and immediate challenge.

Many other tactical approaches may be pursued simultaneously in step with the major thrusts. In general, these must be guided by the principle of denying to the capitalist within the national political economy the right to exploit black labor, whenever the opportune moments arise. Organization of politically oriented labor associations among black employed workers, cementing the bonds among welfare mothers, seeking more self-determination in the running of schools, and strengthening all existing black social and political organizations are necessary tactics in an overall strategy.

Finally, blacks must use their international kinship ties. Recall that black Americans constitute one of the largest African nations in the world, even though they have no African geographical base. The African connection has to be revived and strengthened. Blacks must begin the process of diplomatic negotiations with the nations of the African continent under a plan whereby each nation reserves a block of territory for the unencumbered settlement of black Americans. A general OAU resolution, coupled with specific enabling pacts with each African nation, based on its own peculiar circumstances, may be a method of procedure. At the same time parallel agreements must be undertaken with the national political state of the United States to finance the migration and to provide some additional compensation to both the migrants and to the host nations.

In sum, black Americans stand at the threshold of a worldwide social revolution. Their unique history of suffering and struggle for survival places them in an unparalleled position to be exemplars to the rest of exploited peoples of how a new social order can be consciously fashioned to reflect the perfectibility of the human condition on earth.

NOTES AND SUGGESTED READING

Introduction

A necessary beginning of the study of black political economy is the work of DuBois (1970), especially Chapter XVII. Nowhere else can be found a more incisive indictment of the falsifiers of black history. This work is especially important because it locates most of these propagandists inside the halls of academia.

A complement to DuBois's work is Karenga (1982), especially Chapter 1. Herein is contained a very important statement of the relevance of black studies as a field of study in American institutions of higher learning.

Chapter 1   The general nature of political economy

Adam Smith (1937) represents the best general introduction to the subject. Indeed, his "Introduction and Plan of the Work" postulates a general model of political economy which we have adopted and elaborated in our own work. Smith's Chapter V is the most concise and unambiguous treatment of the role of the political state that we are aware of. Finally, his Chapter 1 lays down a general program for the study of capitalist political economy.

Chapter 2   Special types of political economies

Smith (1937) produced his masterpiece during the historical phase of British mercantile capitalism. The book was a polemic against the misguided policies of the merchant capitalist state which placed too much emphasis on the use of state power to enhance the private domestic accumulation of money capital. As an alternative, Smith proposed in Book III that the development of a solid base in domestic non-money commodity production is an absolutely necessary condition for achieving progressive economic development. Such domestic production, however, must be first grounded in a well organized and productive agricultural sector; afterward domestic production should be expanded to encompass a solid and productive industrial sector, properly articulated with the domestic agricultural sector. Only when these two sectors are fully developed should the private capitalists pursue foreign trade, and this only for purposes of importing goods which are necessary and desirable, but which cannot be produced at home.

This reading of Smith's thesis does not square with much that is pawned off in the modern literature as Smithian theory. Those who would have Smith become the father of conservatism and unbridled *laissez faire* should be guarded against.

Any understanding of different types of political economies cannot be complete without a grounding in Karl Marx (1970). The historical material in Part VIII and the discussion of the general law of capital accumulation in Chapter XXV stand unequalled to this day. It is indeed in this work that we come to understand the natural evolution of capitalist society out of pre-capitalist social formations.

Chapter 3 Special cases of black American political economies

The many types of economic transformations which black Americans have experienced can be best understood within an historical framework. Some representative works which contain such a common framework are Baron (1971), Johnson and Campbell (1981), Karenga (1982), and Wilson (1980).

Baron distinguishes an era of slavery from colonial times to the 1860s; landless peasantry and a transitional phase from the 1860s to World War II; and a wage labor period from World War II to the present. The specific and dominant mode of labor performed by black workers establishes the temporal boundaries of the different eras.

Wilson treats the same data as Baron; however, his distinctive eras are rather blurred by the ambiguous designations "pre-industrial," "industrial," and "modern industrial." In addition, he gives no definition of "race"; and his definition of "class" confounds this concept with the differential income levels among the same class of black wage laborers. Inasmuch as "race" and "class" are the major conceptions of his book, these shortcomings tend to detract from an otherwise meaningful contribution.

Johnson and Campbell concentrate on population changes in various subperiods of the three major eras of black labor.

Karenga covers the same eras, but with a particular emphasis on the political and cultural dimensions of the black experience.

Chapter 4 African origins of black Americans

For the African beginnings we find Hopkins (1973) to be a very useful text. However, one should be very critical of his interpretation of facts.

Notes and suggested reading

He has a rather curious "market" conception of economic activity in Africa prior to the European slave operations.

A number of selections from Ajayi and Espie (1970) give a good flavor of the variety of social organizations out of which black slaves came. An excellent treatment of the same general thesis is Murphy (1972). Rodney (1974) approaches the same material, although from a different overall perspective.

Chapter 5 The system of black slave labor and the rise of capitalism in Western Europe, 1619–1865

For the impact of the slave trade on western European capitalism, Williams (1966) is still among the best sources. Rodney (1974) is not only an excellent source for the African beginnings, but also for the slave operations as well.

Davidson (1961) and Hopkins (1973) are very instructive on the European slave operations. Fox-Genovese and Genovese (1983) is a good contribution to the understanding of the relationship between slavery and the accumulation of merchant capital.

By far the most penetrating analysis of the nature of the slave economy in the British North American colonies and later in the southern United States is the first three chapters of DuBois (1970). Practically anything of significance dealing with this subject matter is either lifted from DuBois or represents honest attempts to extend his work.

A vast literature on slavery has emerged since the late 1960s. Most of these works appear to be dillettantish displays of erudition on the part of the authors; however, they are written from some rather meaningless perspectives as far as blacks are concerned. They concoct problems for solution which obscure the real issues or which play down the harshness of the slave regime. A stellar exception to this is Harding (1981), a most refreshing intellectual experience which must be placed on a level with the DuBois contributions.

Many other books, such as Gates (1960), give accurate and penetrating descriptions of the slave economy.

Chapter 6 The black sharecropping system and the development of capitalism in the United States, 1865–1965

This phase of black labor is best analyzed by DuBois (1970), chapters IV–XVI.

Ransom and Sutch (1977) is an excellent contribution to an overall description of this period. A major problem with the book, however, is the underlying hypothesis that a set of "flawed institutions" which were put into place in the south were the primary causes of southern, and thus, black poverty. This may be generally true. But the obvious corollary that these institutions were deliberately set up as conduits to siphon off the

Notes and suggested reading

wealth produced in the south into the northern capitalist coffers is not at all addressed in any significant way. Furthermore, the outright robbery of black labor by landlords and merchants is treated quite gingerly.

Many other books of a general nature contain useful material for a study of black sharecropping. Gates (1960) and Shannon (1973) are two good examples.

A few books and articles deal with this period within some sort of theoretical framework. The problem with all of them is that in all such cases the authors think they are dealing with blacks as wage laborers. A good example is Higgs (1977). This work uses all kinds of "estimating models" which generate some rather curious interpretations of the facts.

Donald Harris ("Capital Exploitation and Black Labor: Some Conceptual Issues," 1978) represents a pioneering attempt to understand the differential exploitation of blacks in comparison with non-blacks. Fusfeld (1980) extends Harris's theory. In both cases, however, the empirical underpinnings of the theory are more relevant to the sharecropping period. These works are nevertheless important in pointing to the conditions of the period of transition from sharecroppers to wage laborers, a period when blacks were entering the wage labor system in occupations at the fringes of capitalist enterprises.

While Perlo (1976) treats contemporary issues, the work is to be considered an empirical tract which complements Harris.

Chapter 7 The black wage labor system and the rate of capital accumulation in the United States, 1965–

An elaborate and advanced general treatment of capitalist political economy is Harris (*Capital Accumulation and Income Distribution*, 1978).

Brown (1973) has put together some of the most relevant data on wage distribution across many different nations in different periods of history. His reliance on a kind of marginal productivity theory of wages, however, detracts from the importance of the book as a rich source of understanding.

It goes without saying that Marx (1970) and Smith (1937) are the most comprehensive and incisive analyses of wage labor.

Some empirical data on occupational and wage distributions among black laborers are given in Hogan and Harris (1974).

Chapter 8 The role of black Americans in the social reconstruction of the future

An excellent starting point for a discussion of the future is Wilhelm (1970). This is a sharp analysis of the possibilities. Yet it leaves out a most important factor – the deliberate and free will of black workers. Hogan (1972) calls attention to this omission.

Our own attempts throughout the book are seriously flawed in one important respect. It should be obvious that black political economy

Notes and suggested reading

cannot be approached from the narrow perspective of the academic economist. All aspects of life of black people as they survive as a people throughout history should be essential aspects of the study. Their history, language, art, music, religion, family structures, physical make-up, biological needs – all these are essential elements in forging the black condition and should be dealt with in any book on black political economy. My own shortcomings have precluded the use of very important sources in history, anthropology, education, linguistics, sociology, geology, biology, music, art, and a host of other disciplines. This shortcoming should be rectified in future work by black social scientists who seek clarity and understanding of this most important topic.

BIBLIOGRAPHY

Ajayi, J. F. Ade and Ian Espie (eds) (1970), *A Thousand Years of West African History*, Ibadan University Press, Nigeria, 1970.

Baron, Harold (1971), "The Demand for Black Labor: Historical Notes on the Political Economy of Racism," *Radical America*, 5:2.

Brown, Henry Phelps (1973), *The Inequality of Pay*, University of California Press, Berkeley.

Davidson, Basil (1961), *The African Slave Trade: Precolonial History, 1450–1850*, Little, Brown, Boston.

DuBois, W. E. B. (1970), *Black Reconstruction in America, 1860–1880*, Atheneum, New York.

Fox-Genovese, Elizabeth and Eugene Genovese (1983), *Fruits of Merchant Capital: Slavery and Bourgeois Property in the Rise and Expansion of Capitalism*, Oxford University Press, New York.

Fusfeld, Daniel R. (1980), "Capitalist Exploitation and Black Labor: An Extended Conceptual Framework," *Review of Black Political Economy*, 10:3.

Gates, Paul W. (1960), *The Farmer's Age: Agriculture, 1815–1860*, M. E. Sharpe, White Plains, New York.

Harding, Vincent (1981), *There is a River: The Black Struggle for Freedom in America*, Harcourt Brace Jovanovich, New York.

Harris, Donald J. (1978), *Capital Accumulation and Income Distribution*, Stanford University Press.

Harris, Donald J. (1978), "Capitalist Exploitation and Black Labor: Some Conceptual Issues," *Review of Black Political Economy*, 8:2.

Higgs, Robert (1977), *Competition and Coercion: Blacks in the American Economy, 1865–1914*, University of Chicago Press.

Hogan, Lloyd (1972), "Who Needs the Negro," *Review of Black Political Economy*, 3:1.

Hogan, Lloyd and Harry Harris (1974), "The Occupational–Industrial Structure of Black Employment in the U.S.," *Review of Black Political Economy*, 6:1.

Hopkins, A. G. (1973), *An Economic History of West Africa*, Columbia University Press, New York.

Bibliography

Johnson, Daniel M. and Rex R. Campbell (1981), *Black Migration in America: A Social and Demographic History*, Duke University Press, Durham, North Carolina.

Karenga, Maulana (1982), *Introduction to Black Studies*, Kawaida Publications, Inglewood, California.

Marable, Manning (1983), *How Capitalism Underdeveloped Black America*, South End Press, Boston.

Marx, Karl (1970), *Capital*, vol. 1, International Publishers, New York.

Murphy, E. Jefferson (1972), *History of African Civilization: The Peoples, Nations, Kingdoms and Empires from Prehistory to the Present*, Dell, New York.

Perlo, Victor (1976), *The Economics of Racism, U.S.A.: Roots of Black Poverty*, International Publishers, New York.

Ransom, Roger L. and Richard Sutch (1977), *One Kind of Freedom: The Economic Consequences of Emancipation*, Cambridge University Press.

Rodney, Walter (1974), *How Europe Underdeveloped Africa*, Howard University Press, District of Columbia.

Shannon, Fred A. (1973), *The Farmer's Last Frontier: Agriculture, 1860–1897*, M. E. Sharpe, White Plains, New York.

Smith, Adam (1937), *Wealth of Nations*, Modern Library Giant, New York.

U.S. Department of Commerce, Bureau of the Census, *Statistical Abstract of the United States*, USGPO, Washington, D.C.

Wilhelm, Sydney (1970), *Who Needs the Negro*, Schenkman, Cambridge, Massachusetts.

Williams, Eric (1966), *Capitalism and Slavery*, Capricorn Books, New York.

Wilson, William Julius (1980), *The Declining Significance of Race: Blacks and Changing American Insitutions*, 2nd edn, University of Chicago Press.

INDEX

Africa, 6–7, 42, 69, 79; communal society in, 82, 163; feudal society in, 81–2; food as wealth in, 80; labor process in, 82; as origin of black Americans, 6–7, 39, 69, 72, 78–83, 143, 163, 168, 171; pre-capitalist society in, 80–2; racial stocks in, 67; ruling class in, 80, 82; shipment of blacks from, 71, 74, 84, 93, 163; slavery/slave operations in, 80–2, 85–7, 91; trade in, 81; wealth in (15th cent.), 79–81, 82
agricultural wage payment system, 110
American Revolution (American War of National Liberation), 92
Angola, 67
Arab world, 45
aristocracy, 38, 85
armed forces, 63
Atlantic slaving operations, 67, 71, 76, 91, 92; as source of capital in Western Europe, 85–92
Australia, 49

backward linkages in production, 132–3, 138
Barbados, 36, 37
Belize, 36
black capital: accumulation, 142–9, 152, 156; primitive, 156–7; production, 171; see also money/capital
black capitalists, 118, 144, 156–8
Black External Labor, 74, 133–5
Black External Labor Process, 131–6, 141–2, 143–4, 164, 165; see also External Labor Process

black households: consumer goods purchased by, 140–1; demography of, 117–18, 122–3, 127, 163; food purchased by, 127–9; and Internal Labor Process, 139; non-food purchases by, 127–9; quantity of food in, 137
black human energy: capital from, 133; from consumer goods, 130; market for, 120–6, 130–2, 150–1; ownership of, 133–4, 146; and political state, 150–2; production of, in Internal Labor Process, 137–8; see also human energy; labor(ers)/human labor
Black Internal Labor Process, 136–42, 143–4, 147, 160–1, 165, 169; see also Internal Labor Process
black middle class, 158
black-owned business, 157–8, 166
Black Wage Labor System, 34, 164; backward linkages in, 132–3, 138; Black External Labor Process in, 131–6, 141–2, 143–4; and black household demography, 117–18, 122–3; Black External Labor Process in, 136–42, 143–4; black laborer's role in, 145–6; black population in, 145, 147–8; and business firms, 118–19; buyer's role in, 128; capital accumulation/configuration in, 133, 142–9, 152, 154, 161; capitalist's role in, 144–6; capitalist theft in, 148–9; and commodities, 132–3, 150–1; distribution of consumer goods in, 126–9, 137, 139, 143; distribution

Index

Black Wage Labor System (*cont.*)
of money in, 126–7; economic classes in, 117–20; employment in, 120–1, 135–6, 139; exploitation of blacks in, 1–2, 69–70, 74, 75, 77, 114, 115, 123, 142, 146–9, 153, 161, 168–9; External Labor Process in, 116, 119, 128, 164; food as commodity in, 127–8; food requirements in, 129; forward linkages in, 133, 139; household formation in, 139; human energy ownership in, 150–2; industries employing blacks in, 124–6; Internal Labor Process in, 120, 131–2, 152, 164; investments in, 134, 145; jobs available to blacks in, 135–6, 147; market mechanisms in, 143, 148–9, 150–1, 152–3, 164–5; material means of survival in, 147–8, 153; non-black capitalists in, 115–16, 118, 127, 136, 142, 144, 147–8, 151; non-food purchases in, 127–9; and political state, 149–56; production technology of, 118–19; profit-targeting situations in, 128; property rights in, 130, 150; seller's role in, 128; social reproduction in, 149; trade unions in, 126; unemployment in, 120–1, 124, 146–7, 161, 166, 170–1; and US economy, 158; wage distribution/rates in, 120–6, 129, 134, 146–7, 158; wealth accumulation in, 116–17, 156–7; will of the workers in, 122

black wage laborers, 114, 120, 124, 143–6, 168; and capital accumulation, 161; and capitalists, 158–62; and consumer goods market, 160; means of survival of, 130–2; and non-black capitalists, 151; and non-black workers, 159–61, 166, 168; reproduction of, 115, 142, 145, 160–1; unemployment of, 120–1, 124, 146–7, 161

blacks/black Americans: African origins of, 6–7, 39, 69, 72, 78–83, 143, 163, 168, 171; in American capitalist society, 39; births among, 68–9, 73–4; and capitalism, 1, 166; economic development of, 1, 34; employment of, 73–4, 76, 123–6; exploitation of (general discussion), 4–5, 70–2, 75, 145, 166–8; exploitation of, under Black Wage Labor System, 1–2, 69–70, 74, 75, 77, 114, 115, 123, 142, 146–9, 153, 161, 168–9, 171; exploitation of, under capitalism, 64–5, 165–6; exploitation of, under sharecropping labor system, 1–2, 69, 76–7, 102, 143–4; exploitation of, under slavery, 1–2, 69, 76–7, 85, 97–101, 143, 164; geographic domain of, 71; heroes among, 167; historical influences on, 67; in labor unions, 159; land owned by, 75, 170; living standard of, 166; migration of, 41, 110–14, 117, 143, 171; music of, 113; and non-black capitalists, 116; and non-black wage laborers, 115; and political state, 71; population statistics of, 140, 145, 147–8; poverty of, 1, 5, 8, 73, 115, 148, 162; racial identification of, 68–9; reproduction of, as a population, 2–3, 72, 136; reproduction of, as a population, 2–3, 72, 136; reproduction of, as wage laborers, 115, 142, 145, 160–1; revolution of, 167–8; segregation of, 75, 109, 161; as sharecroppers, 39, 41, 71–2, 74, 75; shipment of, from Africa to America, 71, 74, 84, 93, 163; as slaves, 39, 71–2, 74; social reproduction of, 2–5, 70, 76, 142; social revolution of, 75, 167–9, 171; social transformation of, 114; socialization of, 152; supression of, 11; survival of, as a population, 2, 5, 70, 126, 139–40, 166, 168–9; unemployment of, 120–1, 124, 146–7, 161, 166, 170–1; in United States, 39, 73–5, 89–90, 166; and US economy, 141; as wage laborers, 41, 71–3, 74–6, 115; *see also* black wage laborers

Brazil, 42

British North American colonies: crops grown in, 95–6; establishment of, 92; External Labor Process in, 94–7; exports of, 95–6; food supply in, 95; Internal Labor Process in, 95–7; investment in, 93; land grants in,

180

Index

93; political state in, 97; slave operations in, 71, 72, 74, 76–8, 89, 91, 93–4, 97–8; slave population in, 93, 96–7; slave society in, 91; slave system in, 97–9, 100–2; wealth accumulation in, 95–6; *see also* Great Britain

Canada, 36, 49, 71
capital: *see* money/capital; wealth; wealth accumulation
capitalism/capitalist society, 38, 40, 49, 50–66, 84; and black Americans, 1, 166; and black social reproduction, 4; and black wage laborers, 158–62; buyer's role in, 57–60; capital stocks in, 62; capitalist class in, 38–9, 60–3, 86; civil rights in, 63; class basis of, 10, 50; commodities in, 50–2; contradictions in, 65; distribution process in, 58; employment in, 65–6; exploitation of laborers in, 64–5, 165–6; and External Labor, 61, 86; and feudalism, 39; and food supply, 53; in Great Britain, 38, 76; labor processes in, 53, 59–62, 63–6; market forces in, 57–66; money commodity in, 53–4, 56–7, 62, 91; and political state, 56, 59, 62, 65; profit-making cycle in, 90; property in, 53, 57–8; reproduction cycle in, 65–6; seller's role in, 57–60; and sharecropping labor system, 104, 107; and slavery, 86, 88–92, 100–1, 103–4; social reproduction in, 53, 120; unemployment in, 65–6; wage laborers class in, 38–9, 53, 86; wage rate in, 58, 61, 64–5; wealth accumulation in, 61, 65, 66; in Western Europe, 13, 73; worker rebellion in, 63
Carolinas, 93
Caribbean basin/Sea, 71, 84–5, 102; sugar colonies in, 92
Central America, 84, 102
China, 36, 67
CIO (Congress of Industrial Organizations), 159
civil rights: in capitalist society, 63; and political state, 151–2, 155–6
Civil Rights Movement, 75, 113–14

Civil War, 74, 92, 103, 118
commerce, 84
commodity(ies), 50–2; in capitalist society, 50–2, 90; defined, 54; distribution of, *see* market/market institutions; final, 119–20, 125–6; and food, 50, 104; intermediary, 119, 125–6, 128, 132–3, 134; and labor, 50, 54–5; money, 53–7, 62, 90–1; ownership of, 62, 150–1; price of, 52; primary, 119, 125–6, 128, 134; production of, in Black Wage Labor System, 132–3; slave-produced, 101; *see also* consumer goods
communalism, 38–9, 40, 42–3; in Africa, 82, 163
consumer expenditures, 59, 140–1
consumer goods, 59, 64, 120, 128, 133; bill, 123; black expenditures for, 140–1; black, market for, 126–9, 130–2; consumption of, 137; distribution of, 126–7; from human energy, 130–1; market for, 57, 59–61, 160; prices of, 128; *see also* commodity(ies)
Consumer Goods Market, 57, 59–61, 160
consumer sales revenues, 59
cotton, 47, 75, 76, 95, 100–1; as capital, 104, 105; commercialization of, 112; converted into food, 107; in sharecropping labor system, 105–7, 110, 157
covenant agreements, 155
Cuba, 67

demand wage, 121–2
democracy, 66–7
Denmark, 85
Distribution Process(es), 17, 37, 166; in capitalist society, 57; in communal society, 42; for consumer goods, 126–7; for food, 17, 21, 23, 24, 26–8; and labor periods, 33; for money, 126–7; for people, 24–6, 46; of wages, in Black Wage Labor System, 120–6, 129

Eastern Europe, 66–7
El Salvador, 36, 37

181

Index

employment, 10; in Black Wage Labor System, 120–1, 135–6, 139; in capitalist society, 65–6

Europe, 67, 70; capital accumulation from slaving in, 87–8; capitalism in, 86, 88–92; External Labor Process in, 86; feudalism in, 86; slaving operations in, 78–9, 81–3, 86–92

External Labor, 2, 30, 33, 37, 41; black, 74, 133–5; in Black Wage Labor System, 116, 119, 128, 164; cycle of, 25, 27; defined, 5; and human energy, 23–4; input of, 51; intensity of, 22–3, 42, 60; and Internal Labor, 24–6; level and continuity of, 25; number of people engaged in, 22, 25; output of, 52; slave, 94–5, 100, 102, 164; technology of, 132; terms of, set by political state, 153

External Labor Process, 17; activity within, 22; attractive forces of, 25–6; black, 131–6, 141–2, 160, 165–6; black workers and non-black capitalists in, 150; in Black Wage Labor System, 116, 119, 128, 131–6; in British North American colonies, 94–7; in capitalist society, 53, 59–62; in communal society, 42; and conscious will of people, 22; distribution of commodities/material goods in, 6; distribution of people in, 6, 24–6, 30–1; exploitation in, 136; and food production, 21–4, 30–1, 51–2; in feudal society, 46, 48; jobs available to blacks in, 135–6; ownership of, 25–7; and political state, 31–2; resistance within, 25–6, 27; and slavery, 43–4, 86, 164; see also Black External Labor Process

family: extended, 42; formations, 146; in Internal Labor process, 18–19, 138

federal land policy, 103

feudalism/feudal society, 38–40, 45–50, 64; in Africa, 81–2; and capitalism, 39; classes in, 46–50; distribution of people in, 46; External Labor Process in, 48; and food, 46–9; Internal Labor Process in, 48; landlord's role in, 46–9; political state in, 49; produce in, 47; sharing agreement in, 46–8; wealth accumulation in, 48; see also sharecropping labor system

Florida, 112

food: and capital accumulation, 104; in capitalist society, 53; and commodities, 50, 104; as commodity, 127–8; in communal society, 42; consumption of, 16–20, 26–7, 30; creation/production of, 16, 21–4, 30–1, 51–2, 170; cycle and time trend for, 23; distribution of, 17, 21, 23, 24, 26–8; in External Labor Process, 21–4, 30–1, 51–2; excess of, 28; exchange value of, 52; in feudal society, 46, 48–9; from human energy, 16–17; and human population, 29–30; in Internal Labor Process, 30–137; and money, 51; property rights in, 28; reproduction of, in slave labor system, 44–5; self-sufficiency of, 104; in sharecropping labor system, 105; and social reproduction, 21–2; specific value of, 51; stocks, 28; synthesis of, 29; units, 127

forward linkages in production, 133

France, 78, 85, 92

free wage laborers, 114

General Law of Conservation of Labor Input, 62

General Theory, 10

Georgia, 93

Glorious Revolution, 38

government bureaucracy; see political state

Great Britain, 34, 38, 85; capital accumulation from slaving in, 87–8; capitalism in, 38, 76; economy of, 90; manufacturing class in, 85; merchant class in, 85; sugar colonies of, 92; see also British North American colonies

Greece, 45

historical and dialectical materialism, 37–42

historical epochs, 34, 37, 40–2; see also *specific epochs*: capitalism; communalism; feudalism; slavery; socialism

182

Index

human energy: black, *see* black human energy; in capitalist society, 50; consumer goods from, 130–1; creation of, 16–17, 19; demand for, 121; distribution of, 21; food production from, 21–4; from Internal Labor, 61; market for, in Black Wage Labor System, 120–6; market for, in capitalist society, 57–8, 60, 159; private ownership of, in capitalist society, 63; technology of production of, 122; *see also* black human energy; labor(ers)/human labor

human labor; *see* labor(ers)/human labor

human population: defined, 40; distribution of, in labor processes, 24–6; excess of, 28; and External Labor Process, 23–4; and food supply, 29–30; in political economy, 14–16; production of, 20; reproduction of, in slave labor system, 44; size of, 20; social reproduction of, 23; synthesis of, 29

indentured servitude, 93; *see also* slavery/slave labor system

Internal Labor, 2, 30, 33, 37, 41; accumulated black, 140; and commodities, in capitalist society, 51–2; cycle of, 25, 26; defined, 5; and External Labor, 24–6; forms of, 140; and human population, 23; input of, 51, 140–1; intensity of, 19–20, 42, 48; level and continuity of, 27; mode, 139; output of, 52; per capita requirement for generation of, 127; slave, 94, 102, 164; standards of, set by political state, 153; technology of, 123, 137, 141

Internal Labor Process, 17–21; attractive forces of, 25–7; backward linkages in, 138; black, 136–42, 143–4, 147; black capital accumulation in, 142–9; black human energy production in, 137–8; black population in, 137–41; in Black Wage Labor System, 120, 131–2, 152; in British North American colonies, 95–7; in capitalist society, 53, 59–62; in communal society, 42; distribution of commodities/material goods in, 6; distribution of food in, 17–18; distribution of people in, 6, 24–6, 30–1; and family unit, 18–19, 138; in feudal society, 48; and food consumption/production, 18–20, 25, 30–1, 137; forward linkages in, 133, 139; household formation in, 139; and human population, 20–1, 137–41; ownership of, 25–7; and political state, 31–2; and potential population, 88–9; replacement function in, 138–9, 145; resistance within, 25–6; slave, 43, 89, 94, 99, 164; *see also* Black Internal Labor Process

Jamestown, Virginia, 93
Japan, 34, 49

Keynes, John Maynard, 10
ku klux klan, 106, 112, 155
Kuo Min Tang, 67

labor(ers)/human labor: in capitalist society, 53, 60–1; and commodities, 50, 54–5; exchange value of, 52; family, 163; and food, 50; intensity of, 55–6, 66; metric, 55; and money, 51; social, 163; specific labor of, 51–2, 58; standard quantity of, 56; time duration of, 55–6; *see also* human energy; black human energy

labor cycle, *see* External Labor; External Labor Process; Internal Labor; Internal Labor Process

labor unions, 159
land grants, 93
Law of Accumulation of Capital, 62
Law of the Markets, 61–2
Law of Production, 62

manufacturing industry, 103
Mao Tse-tung, 67
Market for Consumer Goods, 57, 59–61
Market for Human Energy, 57–8, 60
market institutions/markets, 9, 52, 54, 164–5; in capitalist society, 57–66; and commodities, 52, 54; distribution, 62–6; and Internal Labor, 52; law of, 61; and political state, 152–3; role of individual in, 10

183

Index

Marshall, Alfred, 9, 10
Marx, Karl/marxism, 38–40, 66, 91
Maryland, 93
material means of survival, 4, 9, 11, 14–16, 139, 141, 166–7, 169–70; in Black Wage Labor System, 147–8, 153; in slave labor system, 44
materialism (historical and dialectical), 37–42
Mexico, 71
Middle Atlantic colonies, 74, 76
monetary theory, 11
money/capital, 50–2, 59; accumulation of, in Black Wage Labor System, 133, 142–9, 152, 154, 161, 168; accumulation of, from slavery, 85–92, 98–101; barrier, 53; black accumulation of, 142–9, 152, 156–7, 171; commodity, 53–7, 62, 90–1; configuration of, 119, 133; defined, 54; exchange value of, 58–9; from human energy, 133; -isoquantity, 55–7; as medium of exchange, 131; merchant, 157; monopoly, 158; nature of, 65; for non-food purchases, 127–9; prices, 130; role of, 54; as Standard Unit of Measure, 56; types of, 119; wage(s), 129, 130; *see also* wealth/Wealth Accumulation
monopoly charters (for slaving), 93
Mozambique, 67

NAACP (National Association for the Advancement of Colored People), 155
National Guard, 63
Netherlands, 78, 85, 95
New Deal, 10
New England, 74, 76, 93
New York, 93
New Zealand, 49
Nicaragua, 67
non-black capitalists, 115–16, 118, 127, 136, 142, 144, 147–8, 151, 153, 159–60; and black capital accumulation, 156; reproduction of, 145
non-black wage laborers, 124, 159, 161, 166, 168
North America, 74, 78, 84, 85, 91–2

Pennsylvania, 93

People's Republic of China, 36, 37
Philippines, 42
pirating, 85, 92
price(s), 10, 59–60
Principles, 9
political economy, 1–2, 9, 24, 34–5, 59; black, 2–3, 70, 72, 76; black sharecropping, 105–10; black slave, 92–8; capitalist, 142, 148–9, 171; characteristics of, 36–7; concept of, 9; continuation of, 6; contradictions in, 39–41; cycle of, 142; defined, 11–13; geographical domain of, 13–14; human labor in, 14–16; influences on, 32–3; micro/macro analysis of, 10; and political state, 10, 31–2; and property relations, 30; and social reproduction, 3–5, 7, 12, 16–17, 28; and time concept, 33–4; and wealth accumulation, 29–31
political state, 41; black employment in, 154; and black unemployment, 154–5; and Black Wage Labor System, 149–56; and blacks, 71, 162; in British North American colonies, 97; and capital accumulation, 152, 154; in capitalist society, 56, 59, 62, 65; and civil rights, 152, 155–6; and exploitation, 156; and External Labor Process, 31–2, 63, 153–4; in feudal society, 49; functions of, 63; and Internal Labor Process, 152, 153; market forces imposed by, 152–3; military and police operations of, 154; and political economy, 10, 31–2; and property rights, 150; racism in, 68; role of, 12; in sharecropping labor system, 109–10, 112; in slave society, 45; wage redistribution programs of, 154; and wealth accumulation, 31–2
population formation period, 88, 97, 137
population production (law of), 20
Portugal, 78, 84–5, 92
Process of Black Capital Accumulation: *see* black capital, accumulation
profit target, 121–2
property: in capitalist society, 53, 57–8; concept of, 25; and political state, 150; private, 12, 50, 52, 57–8,

150; relationships, 27, 30; rights, 28, 150

race/racism, 11, 67–9; concept of, 67–9; in non-black workers, 162; and slavery, 99–9; superiority-inferiority syndrome of, 67–8
replacement function, 138–9, 145
reproduction: of blacks as a population, 2–3, 72, 136; of blacks as wage laborers, 115, 142, 145, 160–1; individual, 3–4, 14–16; of material means of survival, 14–16; of sharecropping political economy, 105–10; social, *see* social reproduction
Republic of New Africa, 170
Roman empire, 45–6
ruling class, 68

secession of slave states, 103
segregation, 75, 109, 161
sharecropping labor system, 6–7, 34, 47–8, 117, 164, 167; beneficiaries of, 108; contradictions in, 110; cotton in, 105–7, 110, 157; crops produced in, 107; defined, 47; distribution process in, 106; exploitation of blacks in, 1–2, 69, 76–7, 102, 143–4; External Labor in, 107, 108, 110, 164; food in, 105; income distribution in, 111; Internal Labor in, 109, 110, 164; land allocation in, 106–7, 111; landlord class in, 106, 108, 110; merchant class in, 105–8, 110; and migration of blacks to southern cities, 110–14; and political state, 109–10, 112; reproduction of sharecroppers, in 108; sharing agreements/contracts in, 106–7, 110; social relations in, 105; wealth accumulation in, 105, 108–9, 110, 156; *see also* feudalism/feudal society; sharecropper(s)
sharecropper(s): as former slaves, 105, 164; population, 109–10; reproduction of, 108; white, 105
slave(s): former, as sharecroppers, 105, 164; freeing of, 103, 164; importation of, 99; as indicator of wealth, 29, 43, 100; masters, 93–7, 99, 101; population, 93, 96–7, 99–100, 102; reproduction of, 79, 88–9, 91, 96, 102; restrictions on, 45; revolt, 94, 167; society, 91, 100; survival of, 88–90
slavery/slave labor system, 6–7, 34, 38, 40, 43–6, 64, 78–9, 97–9, 100–3, 106, 163–4, 167; in Africa, 80–2, 85–7, 91; capital accumulation from, in US, 98–101; capital accumulation from, in Western Europe, 85–92; and capitalism, 86, 88–92, 100–1, 103–4; classes in, 43–6; distribution of slaves in, 43; effect on industries in Europe, 87–8; exploitation of blacks in, 1–2, 69, 76–7, 85, 97–101, 143, 164; External Labor Process in, 43–4, 86, 164; and food, 44–5; income distribution in, 110–11; Internal Labor Process in, 43, 89, 94, 99, 164; means of survival in, 44; motives for, 79; origins of, in communal society, 39; outlawing of, 103; profits from, 79, 90–2, 101; and race relations, 98–9; reproduction of food in, 44; reproduction of human population in, 44; as social organization, 98; wealth in, 29, 43–5, 100, 102; whites in, 99
Smith, Adam, 9, 11–12, 42
social reproduction, 40–1; in Black Wage Labor System, 149; in capitalist society, 53, 120; and food supply, 21–2; of human population, 23; institutional mechanisms of, 16–17, 37, 40, 72; and political economy, 3–5, 7, 12, 16–17, 28; and time concept, 33; *see also* reproduction
social switching mechanism/process, 2, 6
socialism/socialist system, 4, 39, 40, 66–7
South America, 84
Soviet Union, 34, 36–7, 66–7
Spain, 78, 84–5, 92
Special Law of Conservation of Labor Inertia, 62
Special Law of Conservation of Labor Output, 61
supply wage income, 123
Sweden, 85

Index

Tanzania, 67
tariffs, 103
Third World, 37
time: concept of, in political economy, 33–4; historical, 33–4; and labor, 55–6; periodic, 33–4; real, 33–4, 40; and social reproduction, 33
trade unions, 126
transportation network, 103

unemployment: in Black Wage Labor System, 120–1, 124, 146–7, 161, 166, 170–1; in capitalist society, 65–6; and political state, 154–5
United States, 36, 85; black population in, 39, 73–5, 89–90, 166; black sharecropping in, 47–8; black slavery in, 45–6; business firms in, 119; capital accumulation in, from slavery, 98–101; capitalism in, 74; economy of, 115, 120, 141–2, 158; as feudal state, 49; historical epochs of, 34; segregation in, 75, 109, 161; slavery in, *see* British North American colonies
unpaid labor (in Black Wage Labor System), 136

Virginia, 74, 93

wage(s): bill, 121, 128, 146; cost, 58; distribution/rates in Black Wage Labor System, 120–6, 129, 134, 146–7, 158; earning class, 49; income, 58; laboring period, 140; rates, under capitalism, 58, 61, 64–5, 166; redistribution programs, 154
War on Poverty, 156
wealth: in Africa (15th cent.), 79–80; black, 152, 156; as capital, 50; in communal society, 42; defined, 28–9; firearms as, in Africa, 80–1; slaves as indicator of, 29, 43, 100; structure of, 41; *see also* money/capital
Wealth Accumulation, 2, 9, 10, 11, 17, 37; black, 142–9, 152, 156; in Black Wage Labor System, 116–17, 156–7; in British North American colonies, 95–6; in capitalist society, 61, 65, 66; in feudal society, 48; and political economy, 29–31; and political state, 31–2; process of, 28–31, 33; in sharecropping labor system, 105, 108–9, 110, 156; as social switching process, 6; *see also* money/capital
Wealth of Nations, 9
Western Europe, 45, 47, 49, 84; capitalism in, 13, 73; feudalism in, 84; slave colonies of, 92; slaving operations of, 78–9, 85–92
working class, 68; *see also* labor(ers)/human labor